The
Great
Comanche
Raid

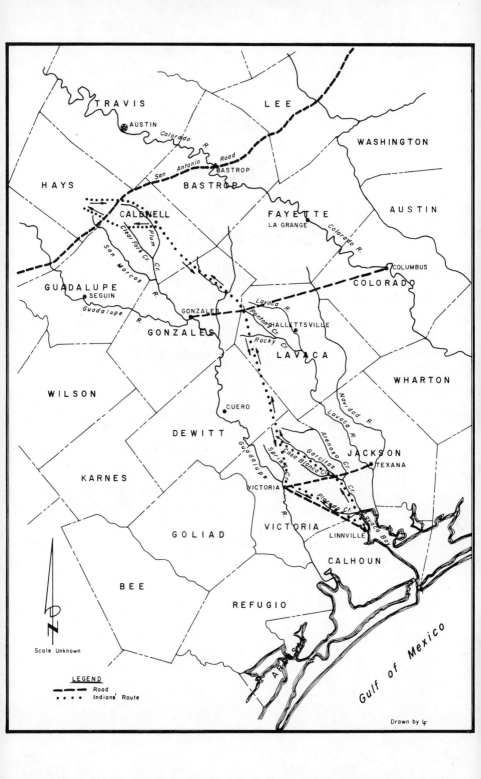

TRAVIS

AUSTIN

LEE

WASHINGTON

Colorado R.

HAYS

San Antonio Road

BASTROP

BASTROP

FAYETTE

LA GRANGE

AUSTIN

CALDWELL

Clear Fork Cr.

Plum Cr.

San Marcos R.

Colorado R.

COLUMBUS

GUADALUPE

SEGUIN

Guadalupe R.

GONZALES

COLORADO

Lavaca R.

Ponton Cr.

HALLETTSVILLE

GONZALES

Rocky Cr.

LAVACA

WILSON

WHARTON

CUERO

Navidad R.

Lavaca R.

DEWITT

Guadalupe R.

Arenoso Cr.

Garcitas Cr.

Spring Cr.

Casa Blanca Cr.

JACKSON

TEXANA

KARNES

VICTORIA

Placedo Cr.

Chocolate Cr.

Lavaca Bay

GOLIAD

VICTORIA

LINNVILLE

CALHOUN

BEE

REFUGIO

Gulf of Mexico

Scale Unknown

LEGEND
▬ ▬ Road
• • • • Indians' Route

Drawn by LF

The Great Comanche Raid

Boldest Indian Attack of the Texas Republic

Donaly E. Brice

EAKIN PRESS ★ Austin, Texas

FIRST EDITION

Copyright © 1987
By Donaly E. Brice

Published in the United States of America
By Eakin Press, P.O. Box 23069, Austin, Texas 78735

ISBN 0-89015-594-1

Library of Congress Cataloging-in-Publication Data

Brice, Donaly E.
    The great Comanche raid.

    Based on the author's thesis (masters — Sam Houston State University)
    Bibliography: p.
    Includes index.
    1. Comanche Indians — Wars, 1840–. 2. Indians of North America — Texas
— History. 3. Texas — History — Republic, 1836–1846. I. Title.
E83.837.B74   1987   976.4'04   87-6770
ISBN 0-89015-594-1

To my wife
Clare Corrington Brice
and to the memory of my parents
Don R. and Arthurine E. Brice
this book is dedicated

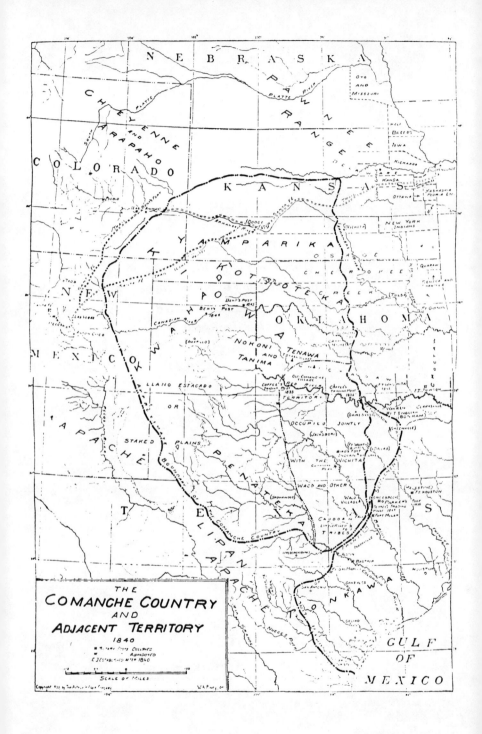

THE
COMANCHE COUNTRY
AND
ADJACENT TERRITORY
1840

Contents

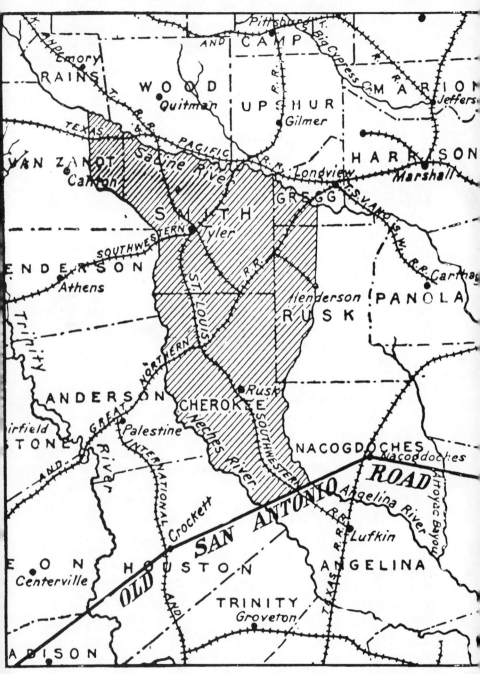

Map of Cherokee Land Grant

Foreword

Just when you become comfortable in your knowledge of the history of a time or place or event, a scholar comes along who looks more deeply into that time or place or event and, as a result, both broadens your knowledge of and changes your perspective on the subject. If you thought you knew the full story of the relations (sometimes trusting, usually not) between the Texians and the Indians during the period of the Republic of Texas, then Donaly Brice will enhance your fund of information and, in the process, deepen your understanding of this important facet of Texas history.

This work began as a thesis which earned the master's degree for its author. Through the years, many observers have been skeptical of master's theses and doctoral dissertations because, as J. Frank Dobie once put it so colorfully, the bulk of them do no more than transfer bones from one graveyard to another. These writings, he implies, normally develop little, if any, new information, rarely produce new insight to sharpen our understanding, commonly are presented in a way that tells a story with all the life squeezed out of it, or a combination of these.

Such is not always the case. This work on the Great Comanche Raid of 1840 demonstrates the value of the thesis. Here is gathered and presented substantially greater information than we previously had at hand concerning this event which, though relatively brief in duration, produced notable effects of lasting significance in the history of our state. Yet despite the importance of the event, no renowned author or teller of tales looked into this subject before Donaly, then a graduate student. What is more, the thirst for knowledge and the pleasure experienced in the historical quest that the master's work began for Donaly did not let him rest until he had shaped his thesis into a book, this book.

Far from being a sterile process, the work of thesis and dissertation writing clearly and substantially enhances the knowledge of our history and ourselves. If you still doubt that academic research and writing produces results well justifying the activity, just read on.

DAVID B. GRACY II
Governor Bill Daniel Professor in Archival
Enterprise, University of Texas at Austin

Acknowledgments

As a boy roaming over the land where the Battle of Plum Creek took place near Lockhart, I remember dreaming of someday writing a book on the Great Comanche Raid. Over the years I continued to collect information on the subject until I had compiled enough material to complete a thesis, "The Great Comanche Raid of 1840: Its Causes and Results," which partially fulfilled the requirements for my graduate degree at Sam Houston State University. The three men who served as my thesis committee, Dr. Oliver M. Refsell, Dr. John W. Payne, and Dr. Elton M. Scott, deserve a debt of gratitude for their guidance and assistance in what was to become the nucleus for this book.

It is not possible to name every person who in some way helped or supported me in this literary effort, for they were many. However, there are a number of individuals who merit special recognition for giving of their time and talents to help me fulfill this endeavor.

A special thanks goes to Michael R. Green, reference archivist at the Texas State Archives in Austin, for his encouragement and constructive criticism throughout the writing of the manuscript. His invaluable knowledge of Texas history has been a great benefit to my effort.

My sincere appreciation is extended to Dr. David B. Gracy II, professor in the Graduate School of Library and Information Science at The University of Texas at Austin, for sharing his time to review my manuscript and contribute the complimentary remarks in the foreword of this book.

To John Anderson of the Texas State Archives, whose

photographic expertise provided an asset which greatly contributed to this book, I offer my thanks for a job well done.

Linda Fields of Austin deserves special recognition for her talent and her contribution of several specially designed maps which enhance the geographical logistics of many of the events described within the text.

Deep appreciation is extended to Ed Gearke, assistant curator of the Alamo Museum in San Antonio, and Susan L. Meyn, curator of ethnology at the Cincinnati Museum of Natural History in Cincinnati, Ohio, for their efforts in locating several artifacts that relate to events detailed in this book.

Particular thanks are due the staff at the Barker Texas History Center, University of Texas Archives, and especially Ralph Elder, who has always been available to assist me enthusiastically with any request that I might have of him.

I wish to acknowledge Laura Saegert of the Texas State Archives for providing a fine index to this book.

To the entire staff of the Texas State Archives I wish to express my appreciation for your helpful assistance, your confidence and, oftentimes, your forbearance. I am sure there were times that you wished those Indians had never made that raid in 1840.

Finally, and most importantly, I wish to express my deepest appreciation and love to my wife, Clare Corrington Brice, for her patience and understanding. Her encouragement as she has stood beside me, and sometimes behind me pushing, has made *The Great Comanche Raid* a reality.

Introduction

The Great Comanche Raid of 1840 was the boldest and most concerted Indian depredation in the history of Texas. This raid resulted in two of the bloodiest and most significant Indian battles Texas ever witnessed. To understand the reasons for this destructive raid upon the settlers of the Texas frontier it is necessary to look back to the early years of the Republic of Texas. During the first administration of Sam Houston, practically no Indian trouble existed because of Houston's understanding and benevolent action toward the Indians. Houston realized that to establish a stable government, it was necessary to make and keep peace with the Indians and the Mexicans. Not all of the leaders in Texas shared Houston's views. Many believed that the Indians and Mexicans should be dealt with more harshly. Such were the feelings of Houston's successor, Mirabeau B. Lamar. On December 9, 1838, Lamar delivered his inaugural address to the Congress of the Republic of Texas. In that address Lamar stated that

> the outlying settlers were continually exposed to predatory aggression on the part of Mexican banditti and the barbarous warfare waged by hostile Indians; that moderation extended to the natives had been followed by the perpetration of atrocious cruelties; a merciful policy had only acted as an

1

incentive to savage tribes to persevere in their barbarities, and it was time that an exterminating war was opened against them, which would "admit to no compromise, and have no termination except in their total extinction, or total expulsion." [1]

Lamar was only partially correct in his accusations against the Indians. Few tribes would attack without provocation or without reason; the majority of the Indians in Texas never posed a major problem so long as they were not molested.

There was a great change in the Texas Indian policy from 1838 to 1839. Houston wanted to live at peace with the Indians, and Lamar wanted to wage a war of extermination against them. This aggressive action taken against the Indians by the Lamar administration was the basic foundation for the Great Comanche Raid of 1840.

Early in his life, Lamar had developed an enmity for Indians. This belligerent attitude was nurtured under the tutelage of Georgia Governor George M. Troup, for whom Lamar served as private secretary. During this tenure, a bitter struggle raged between the state of Georgia and the federal government concerning the removal of Creek and Cherokee Indians from lands that the Indians rightfully claimed.[2] As the cotton South continued its rapid expansion, more insistent demands were made upon the federal government to remove the Indians from lands desired by Southern planters. Through fraudulent methods, the Creeks were duped into ceding all their Georgia lands. A treaty signed at Indian Springs and ratified by the Senate was quickly repudiated by a vast majority of the Creek Nation. President John Quincy Adams aroused many ill feelings when he, "on investigation, found that the treaty had been obtained by fraud, refused to proclaim it in effect, and ordered that new negotiations should be begun." [3] This delay in the acquisition of the coveted Indian lands, along with the federal government dictating its authority of the States Rightists, prompted Lamar to organize the state militia to resist the dictates of Washington and left a lasting effect on his attitudes regarding the Indians.[4]

Lamar's anti-Indian policy in Texas was first initiated

against the Cherokees. This tribe, under the leadership of Chief Bowles, emigrated from the United States into Texas about 1824 and settled in East Texas "on a tract of land along the Angelina, Neches, and Trinity rivers, where they remained for fifteen years."[5] The land upon which the Cherokees resided was very beautiful and was desired by the many settlers moving into Texas. In 1839 the Texas government received information that the Cherokees, along with other tribes, were involved in an alliance with the Centralist party in Mexico. This Mexican-Indian alliance was devised for the purpose of waging war on the settlers of Texas — either to kill them or drive them from the territory. Until Mexico could send a force large enough to retake Texas, the alliance was designed to keep the Texans from establishing a strong foothold. Reports of these intrigues, although greatly exaggerated by Lamar and others among the anti-Indian faction, provided the excuse they needed to expel the Cherokees. In July 1839 the Cherokees were defeated and pushed from Texas.[6]

The line of frontier settlements by 1840 extended southward from Fort Johnson, on the Red River, to near Corpus Christi. The frontier line ran through Bonham, Groesbeck, and the territory just north of Austin and San Antonio. The land north and west of this line was considered Indian territory and was uninhabited except by the Comanches and other hostile tribes.[7]

Settlers on the western frontier were continually harassed by Indian depredations. Several treaties had been made with the Comanches, but none of them were lasting. In January 1840 a council for peace talks was arranged between the Texans and the Comanches. On March 19 the Indians arrived in San Antonio. During the negotiations, a disagreement arose and fighting erupted. In the massacre which followed, thirty-five Comanches were killed, including a number of their principal chiefs.[8]

In August the infuriated Comanches, encouraged by Mexican agents, began their infamous Great Comanche Raid. The Indians moved down through the settlements to Victoria. After attacking the town, killing a number of people and stealing a large number of horses and mules, the Comanches pro-

ceeded toward Linnville. The Indians burned and looted the
stores and warehouses and then began a slow retreat toward
their camps in the Texas Hill Country.(CH. 4)
    On August 12 several Texan forces, under Maj. Gen.
Felix Huston, defeated the Comanches at Plum Creek near
Lockhart. Following this battle, Col. John H. Moore led an
expedition against the Comanches on the upper Colorado
River. The expedition was a success; an entire Comanche village was destroyed and all of the Indians were either killed or
captured.(CH. 6)
    These Texan victories brought a crushing defeat to the
most hostile Indian tribe in Texas. The Comanches were
never able to pose another major threat to the settlers of the
South Central Texas region. After the Indians' defeat, only
minor skirmishes and forays occurred in the region.(CH. 7)

☆ 1

Mexican Intervention Into Indian Affairs

For several years after the Texas Revolution, the country of Mexico was subjected to turbulent conditions. A major struggle for power had developed between the Federalist and Centralist factions of the government. Although the Centralists were in power, their position was somewhat unstable. Matters worsened for the Centralists when the French government sent an ultimatum to the bankrupt Mexican government demanding payment on some claims that had been left unpaid. Using the situation to their advantage, the Federalist party began a revolt against the Centralists. This revolution failed, and "the usual shooting of the generals in charge followed." [1]

Mexico's foreign and domestic problems prevented the country from raising a force large enough to return to the north and regain Texas from the Americans. Not wanting the Texans to have the advantage of consolidating their independence, the Centralists began formulating the idea of an Indian-Mexican alliance to retard colonization and eventually to retake Texas and drive the settlers from the territory. Although there is no substantial evidence to prove that Mexican agents were attempting to incite the Indians to wage war on the settlers in 1836, there were several reports of Mexican agents circulating among the Indian tribes.

Even before Texas secured her independence with the final shots at San Jacinto, there was great apprehension among the people of Texas concerning the imminent threat of Indian uprisings instigated, in part, by Mexican emissaries sent by a government bent on pushing the Anglo-Americans from its territory. This situation, coupled with the sanguinary defeats of William B. Travis at the Alamo and James W. Fannin in the Goliad campaign, precipitated a state of panic. Houston's ragged Texas army was in full retreat eastward, and thousands of settlers were abandoning their homes and fleeing toward the Sabine River and safety in Louisiana.

With such chaotic conditions existing in Texas, Maj. Gen. Edmund P. Gaines, commander of the western department of the United States Army at Natchitoches, Louisiana, was ordered to execute whatever measures would be necessary to prevent any Mexican force from penetrating the neutral territory between the Neches and Sabine rivers, the disputed boundary between Mexico and the United States. Gaines was also instructed to keep the Indians "in bounds" and prevent them from assisting the Mexican forces. Gaines interrogated numerous persons in an effort to determine the state of affairs in regard to the Indian problem. On April 12, 1836, Miguel de Cortínez testified before General Gaines that his brother Eusebio held a commission from Gen. Martín Perfecto de Cos for the purpose of obtaining Indian allies. Lt. Joseph Bonnell reported to Gaines that during 1836 both Manuel Flores and José María Medrano were circulating among the Indians in an attempt to secure Indian allies for Mexico.[2] Although some of the information gathered by General Gaines was exaggerated or false, rumors of Indian unrest presented Gaines with a pretext for moving his military forces into a favorable position so that he could protect the Anglo-Texan settlers as well as American interests in Texas. In April, Gaines moved part of his command to the Sabine River and established Camp Sabine. However, news of Houston's victory at San Jacinto, along with the easing of an immediate Indian threat, prompted Gaines to halt his westward advance into the neutral ground between Texas and the United States.

In December of 1836 a party of Cherokees arrived in Matamoros to discuss the possibilities of warfare against the Texans. While the Indians were in the city, five Texas prisoners escaped from the Matamoros jail. The Cherokees pursued the group and returned three of the prisoners to the Mexican authorities. The United States consul in Matamoros reported that the Cherokees were no doubt in the actual service of the Mexican government.[3]

In 1837 the existence of an Indian-Mexican alliance became more apparent. During the summer months, a Cherokee delegation visited the Mexican officials in Matamoros to discuss in more detail the particulars of their alliance.[4] It was suggested that the Indians were to assemble north of the San Antonio road between San Antonio and Nacogdoches. When the Indians were ready, Gen. Vicente Filisola was to cross the Rio Grande River with 5,000 troops and march eastward while the Indians moved westward. In this manner the settlers would be driven from Texas. For their part in this military operation the Cherokees were

> to be given and guaranteed possession of their hunting grounds in Texas; a sort of Indian buffer state was to be set up between the Mexican nation and the Americans of the United States.[5]

In his message to the Texas House of Representatives on May 5, 1837, Sam Houston reported that the government of the republic had been informed by "sources entirely satisfactory" of the meeting between the Cherokees and the Mexican officials. He also stated that the Indians promised the Mexican government "three thousand warriors well armed, so soon as it would invade Texas." [6] Although this well-formulated plan was never put into effect, efforts to coordinate Indian and Mexican opposition to the Anglo-Texans continued.

On July 19, 1838, Vicente Cordova, a Mexican citizen residing in Nacogdoches, dispatched a letter to Manuel Flores informing him that Cordova held a "commission from General Filisola, to raise the Indians as auxiliaries to the National Army." Cordova stated that he had already begun his mission by "inviting a meeting of the neighboring tribes." The Cherokees, he said, "promised me to unite as soon as possible for action." [7]

Several other events in 1838 increased suspicions that the Cherokees, as well as other Indian tribes, were involved in a plot to expel all the Texas settlers and help Mexico regain her lost territory. On May 29 a group of "72 citizens, 2 Indians, 34 soldiers of La Bahia, and 20 Cherokee and Caddo Indians" left Matamoros to recruit allies among the Indian tribes of East Texas.[8] Throughout the month of July the group, led by Don Pedro Julian Miracle, slowly made its way across Texas. On August 20, at the mouth of the Caney on the Red River, Miracle was killed by a river pilot and interpreter who had been employed by D. A. G. Wright, a local citizen.[9] A diary with a running account of the group's actions and movements from May 29 to August 20 was found in the possession of Miracle. From the diary's contents the Texans learned that Miracle had visited the Choctaws, Cherokees, Kickapoos, Kichai, Chickasaws, Caddoes, Wacos, Tahuacanos, as well as Cordova in Nacogdoches. Miracle had not only been ordered to relate Filisola's instructions to the Indians but was to distribute powder, lead, and tobacco among the tribes. According to his diary, Miracle was successful in accomplishing his mission before he was killed.[10] It was suspected that, at the time of his death, he was en route to consult with the various tribes in Arkansas about uniting with those in Texas for the purpose of concerting their efforts against the Texans.[11]

Although Miracle succeeded in contacting a number of tribes on his journey through Texas, there is no evidence to indicate that the Indians did much more than politely listen to him. On the contrary, his diary reflects his frustration for the lack of enthusiasm on the part of the Indians and his inability to successfully communicate with them through his interpreters.[12]

On August 7, 1838, Capt. John Durst reported to Maj. Gen. Thomas J. Rusk, the commander of the Texas Militia, that a party of over one hundred armed Mexicans, led by Vicente Cordova and Nathaniel Norris, was camped on the Angelina River. Other reports stated that a number of Biloxi and Ioni Indians accompanied the group of malcontents.

While Rusk ordered a company of soldiers to the Angelina River and called for 200 additional volunteers, President Houston cited the Mexicans and Indians as enemies of the Republic and ordered them to return home. In a reply to Houston's proclamation, Cordova's forces expressed their grievances against the government of the Republic and refused to comply with his orders.

By August 10 Cordova was supported by 300 Indians, as well as a considerable number of defiant Mexicans. These rebels began moving in the direction of the Cherokee Nation. While a group of volunteers under the command of Maj. Henry W. Augustine followed Cordova's trail, Major General Rusk moved directly toward the Cherokees' village confident that Cordova was planning to proceed to the Cherokee Nation and combine his forces with the tribe of Chief Bowles. This assumption proved false when Rusk was informed that Cordova had changed directions and was heading for the upper Trinity. It was also reported that the majority of Cordova's forces had dispersed and fled.[13]

On October 14, 1838, Rusk received word that Cordova and a number of his followers had gathered and joined with the Kickapoo Indians, who were located in present-day Anderson County. Rusk immediately proceeded for the Kickapoo village; on October 16, he was attacked by the Indians. After a short struggle, Rusk made a countercharge and routed the Indians. Eleven Indians were killed, and eleven of Rusk's men were wounded. Following the battle, Cordova's followers had several more skirmishes with the Texas volunteers.[14]

In one of these engagements the Texan forces under General Rusk pursued a band of marauding Caddo Indians across the Texas-United States border. Although the Caddoes were captured and turned over to the Indian agent at Shreveport, this incident created some international tension between the United States and the government of the Republic of Texas because Rusk had not obtained prior permission before crossing into United States territory.[15]

In February 1839, Gen. Valentin Canalizo arrived in Matamoros and succeeded General Filisola as commandant of the northern forces. Canalizo immediately issued instructions to Manuel Flores and many of the Indian tribes in Texas. The instructions, similar to the ones issued by Filisola to Flores and Cordova, called for the Indians to carry out an incessant war against the Texans. He explained that because of troubles with France, Mexico was not presently able to dispatch a force large enough to regain Texas. The Indians were instructed

> not to cease to harass the enemy for a single day — to burn their habitations, to lay waste their fields, and to prevent them assembling in great numbers, by well-concerted movements . . .[16]

The Indians were also directed to "spare the defenseless of all ages and sexes . . ." as well as "punish all Indians friendly to the whites, and all the Mexicans who traded with the whites." They were cautioned not to venture too close to the frontier of the United States, but were advised to "occupy the line of Bexar about the Guadalupe, and from the Leon to the mouth of the San Marcos." By occupying such a line, the Indians would be able to have their enemy in their front and a "friendly and generous nation, as Mexico, in the rear." [17]

After receiving General Canalizo's instructions in March, Cordova and sixty-four Mexicans, Indians, and Negroes set out for Mexico to meet with Canalizo and discuss their plans in detail.[18] Although an effort was made to avoid all contact with the Texas settlers, Cordova's trail was discovered by George W. Davis and Reuben Hornsby. Fearing the trail to have been made by hostile Indians, the men sounded the alarm to the Waterloo settlement (present-day Austin).[19]

On March 27, Col. Edward Burleson of Bastrop received "intelligence of a large body of Indians being encamped at the foot of the mountains on the Colorado" and immediately raised a force of seventy-nine men to protect the settlers of the region. Scouts reported that the trail had crossed the Colorado River and led toward Seguin. Burleson's group immediately set out in pursuit of their enemy.[20] While camping ten miles southwest of Austin, Burleson received a dispatch which reported that a trail of a large Indian party had been found near the Waterloo settlement. This report caused the abandonment of the pursuit of Cordova. On their return to the settlement the men discovered that the trail was not made by Indians but was the same one Burleson's men had followed the day before. Although some of the men were dissatisfied and refused to "take up the trail again," Burleson and about seventy-five men proceeded toward Seguin.[21] While camping on Bear Creek southwest of Austin, a man named Robison, who had deserted Cordova's group, arrived at Burleson's camp and informed the Texans that they were following a band of Mexicans and not Indians. He stated that Cordova was on his way to Matamoros to "obtain munitions of war with which to equip the Indians for the purpose of making a well directed warfare upon the Texans." [22]

Burleson's spies sighted Cordova's group on March 28 and reported their observations. The Mexicans had halted on Mill Creek, near the Guadalupe River, and were resting on the grass, unaware of the approaching Texans. This spot, known today as Battleground Prairie, is located about five miles east of Seguin.[23] In preparing to attack the Mexicans, Burleson divided his forces into two divisions. The right wing was commanded by Capt. Micah Andrews and the left wing by Capt. Jesse Billingsley. The Texans formed a spearhead, and the order was given to attack. The Mexicans, caught completely off guard, immediately fled. A running battle of five or six miles ensued. Approximately eighteen of Cordova's men were killed and several were taken prisoner. A large number of Mexicans were wounded, including Cordova. According to John Wesley Wilbarger, who obtained his information from two participants in this fight, the Texans had no losses.[24]

Burleson's official report to Lamar on April 4, 183[8], reported that thirty of Cordova's men were killed and nineteen were captured. The bodies of the dead were found the following day on the battlefield.[25] Although neither Wilbarger nor Burleson reported any casualties among the Texans, Andrew Sowell states that three Texans were wounded.[26]

After the fight, Dr. James Fentress, who had personally killed one of the Indians in Cordova's party, cut off the head of the slain warrior and carried the gruesome trophy home for "medical examination." [27]

Following this skirmish, Cordova and the remainder of his group made their way on to Mexico. It was soon learned that Cordova was to return to East Texas shortly and would supply the Indian tribes there with arms and ammunition from the Mexican government. Having received this intelligence, a com-

pany of about twenty men led by Capt. Micah Andrews was organized to patrol the western frontier, protect the settlers from
Indian attacks, and keep a lookout for Cordova.

In May 1839 a group of thirteen Mexicans and eleven Indians led by Manuel Flores began traveling along the Texas
frontier to visit the "Northern Indians" and enlist their support in Canalizo's plan.[28] Second in command to Flores was
Ensign Juan de la Garza, who also held a special commission
from General Canalizo to enlist the friendly tribes into the
service of the Mexican government.[29] On May 14, while between San Antonio and Seguin, the Flores group murdered
four surveyors whom they had encountered. The sounds of
their gunfire attracted the surveyors' friends who were
nearby, and the incident was immediately reported to Colonel
Burleson, who hastily assembled a group of volunteers and set
out in pursuit of the enemy.[30]

The next day Flores and his group crossed the Guadalupe River at present-day New Braunfels and moved in the direction of Austin. Late in the afternoon Flores and his party
were sighted by two men of Captain Andrews's company who
had been out looking for a deer to kill for supper. Because it
was late in the day, the men were unable to determine if the
horses they had seen were mounted. They reported their
sighting and Andrews decided to intercept the "unknown
party." On the following day, after a hard pursuit, Andrews
and his men caught up with Flores just as the Mexicans and
Indians entered a dense cedar brake. The groups met face to
face at a distance of fifty yards, but after much discussion over
the size of Flores's group, Andrews decided to return home without a fight. Flores continued north while Andrews and his men
headed for the Waterloo settlement. As the Texans began their
return trip, there was much dissension among the troops as to
whether they should turn around and continue their pursuit or
return without a fight. They finally agreed that the Flores group
was not as large as it had first appeared; so they resumed their
chase. On the seventeenth Captain Andrews's horse became
lame and Andrews was forced to abandon the chase. Several
others were forced to turn back for the same reason.

Lt. James O. Rice was placed in command of the seventeen remaining Texans. On reaching the San Gabriel River on the eighteenth, the Texans found where the enemy had rested and had cut down a bee tree to obtain some honey. Very shortly the Texans came within sight of the Mexicans and Indians. The fleeing enemy attempted several times to "make a stand as if they intended to offer battle," but the Texans did not hesitate and Flores's group would "renew their flight." At the North San Gabriel River the Texans overtook the enemy, and Flores and two of his men were shot and killed. The remainder of the group fled in the direction of the Brazos River, leaving all their supplies and baggage behind. The Texans captured

> about three hundred pounds of powder, and about the same of lead, ready to run into balls and shot, and some bar-lead; they also took one hundred and fourteen head of mules and horses, and all their packing apparatus.[31]

In addition to the munitions and supplies taken from the Flores party, several important papers were found and were forwarded to Colonel Burleson, who reported them to the secretary of war. One of these papers was a letter written by General Canalizo to the chiefs of the Caddoes, Seminoles, Kickapoos, and Cherokees. The letter urged the Indians to follow Flores's instructions and expect nothing from the Texans who were

> greedy adventurers for land, who wish to deprive you even of the sun which warms and vivifies you, and who will not cease to injure you while the grass grows and the water flows.[32]

Another letter found in the possession of Flores was written by Cordova, which stated that he was unable to return to Texas at the present time because of a wound he had received. This wound was probably sustained in his fight with the Texans near Seguin on March 28.[33] With Cordova detained south of the Rio Grande and Flores dead, the Texas settlers hoped to have less trouble with the Indians.

On December 14, 1837, a new land law was enacted which facilitated the acquisition of free land in Texas. This act not only brought about the reorganization of the General

Land Office but also established a board of land commissioners for each county. Through these local boards, claimants could easily obtain grants of land. However, no "African, or Indian, or descendant of either, or any person under the age of sixteen" was allowed to participate in the surveying of public lands.[34] After the passage of this law, the Indians saw their land gradually diminish. They therefore needed little agitation from the Mexicans to induce them to make war on the settlers of Texas. Much of the land desired by the settlers in East Texas was occupied by the Cherokees. After acquiring the papers which had been in the possession of Manuel Flores, President Lamar and his cabinet were convinced that the Cherokees had been in "treasonable correspondence" with the Mexican government. Lamar felt that the Cherokees must be removed from the boundaries of the Republic in order to provide security against an Indian-Mexican plot to retake the territory. By removing the Indians, Lamar realized that prime lands could be opened to Anglo settlement. During the summer of 1839, he began negotiating for a peaceful removal of the Cherokees from Texas.

☆ 2

Expulsion of
the Cherokees

It is a well-established fact that President Lamar's attitude toward the Indians was hostile. Having been influenced by Governor Troup of Georgia during the Creek Wars, Lamar believed that the Indians in Texas, if permitted to remain on their lands, must be subject to the laws of the Republic. On December 21, 1838, Lamar made clear in his first address to Congress that the policy of pacification supported by President Houston had been a total failure. He stated that as long as the Texans pursued such a policy, "so long will the Indians continue to bloody the edge of the tomahawk, and move onward in the work of rapacity and slaughter." [1] Lamar's only answer to the continuous depredations in Texas was that

> we should retaliate their warfare, not in the murder of their women and children, but in the prosecution of an exterminating war upon their warriors, which will admit of no compromise and have no termination except in their total extinction, or total expulsion. [2]

With such an attitude toward the Indians, Lamar, on December 21, 1838, signed a bill that provided for the protection of the northern and western frontiers of Texas. At the same time, this act was to provide for offensive operations against the Indians. The law called for the establishment of a regi-

15

ment of 840 men, who would be enlisted for a period of three years to patrol and protect the frontiers of Texas. From the Kiamisha Red River to the Nueces River a military road was to be constructed. Along this road forts were to be built for added protection against the Indians.[3] The measures provided by this act proved to be inadequate for the protection of the entire Texas frontier, so on December 29, 1838, Lamar signed another bill calling for the formation of eight companies of mounted volunteers. These men were to serve for a period of six months at a time.[4]

Since the anti-Indian sentiment of Lamar was also shared by Gen. Albert Sidney Johnston, the secretary of war, and George W. Bonnell, the commissioner of Indian affairs, war between the settlers and the Indians seemed almost inevitable. By May 1839 the Cherokee situation had reached a climax. There had been much dispute during the past several years over the legality of the claims of the Cherokees for the land on which they were living. According to Chief Bowles, a treaty negotiated between the Provisional Government and the Cherokees on February 20, 1836, gave his tribe legal claim to the land on which they lived. Lamar argued that the treaty "was a nullity when made — is inoperative now; — has never been sanctioned by this Government, and never will be." [5] Although the Cherokees had emigrated to Texas and had settled upon lands which were not their own, the government of the Republic had permitted them to remain there so long as they abided by the laws of the Republic and did not commit depredations on the settlers of Texas. With the mounting evidence that entangled the Cherokees in a conspiracy with the Mexican government and other Indian tribes, Lamar dispatched a letter to Chief Bowles informing him that the government of the Republic was aware of the Indians' dealings with the Mexicans. He further expressed his hope to negotiate a peaceful removal of the Cherokees from Texas since their presence would no longer be tolerated. In his letter, Lamar also charged that the Cherokees had been in "treasonable correspondence" with the Mexican government, had "given countenance" to Cordova's rebellion in August 1838, and had allowed their village to be the meeting place

where our enemies have met to concert their plans, and we
believe that it has been partly through your tribe, that other
Indians with whom we are at war, have received their ammunition and supplies.[6]

Because of the circumstances surrounding the presence of
the Cherokees, President Lamar ordered Maj. B. C. Waters
and a detachment of volunteers to proceed to the Great Saline
and construct a fort in the vicinity of the Cherokee Nation.
Following the group's arrival at the Saline, Chief Bowles
challenged Waters and threatened to attack his troops if an
attempt was made to build a fort in the area. Not wanting to
precipitate a battle with the Cherokees, Major Waters
moved his troops from the Saline. Lamar, receiving news of
the chief's actions, ordered Major Waters to return. He also
dispatched a letter to the Cherokees informing them that
the fort was to be built only for the purpose of preventing
hostile Indians and Mexican agents from circulating in the
area and making their headquarters in the Cherokee Nation. The fort was for the protection of the Texas settlers
and in no way was to inhibit the lifestyle or obstruct the
movement of the Cherokees.[7]

In response to Lamar's demand that the Cherokees be removed from Texas, Chief Bowles agreed that the Indian and
the white man would never be able to live compatibly. He said
the Cherokees would be willing to leave the Republic provided
that the government would compensate them for improvements made upon their lands.[8] Pleased to hear that Bowles
was willing to remove his tribe peacefully, President Lamar
gladly accepted the chief's terms. He immediately appointed
David G. Burnet, James S. Mayfield, Thomas J. Rusk, Albert
S. Johnston, and I. W. Barton as commissioners to negotiate
the removal of the Cherokees to Arkansas.[9]

President Lamar made it known that if the commissioners failed to bring about a peaceful removal of the Cherokees,
it would become necessary to remove the tribe forcibly. For
this reason Col. Edward Burleson, commanding two companies, was ordered to the Cherokee territory. Maj. W. J. Jones
and 200 volunteers were also ordered to the negotiations. Gen.
Kelsey H. Douglass, who also led about 200 men, was placed

in command of the entire operation. The combined forces consisted of approximately 900 men.[10]

According to Albert Sidney Johnston, the commissioners and the Indians attempted for several days to arrange "an equitable basis for the peaceful removal of the Cherokees." The improvements made on the Indians' lands were to be appraised, and the Cherokees were to be paid "in silver and goods before their removal." The commissioners used "every means to effect a friendly negotiation, but without success, and at noon on the 15th day of July announced their failure." [11]

Finding that peaceful negotiations for the Cherokees' removal had been a failure, the militia was ordered to use forceful measures as its only alternative. In accordance with Lamar's orders, on July 15 the militia began its march to the Cherokee village on the Neches River. Col. Willis H. Landrum crossed the Neches and proceeded up the west bank of the river, while the volunteers under Burleson and Rusk directed their march to the camp of Chief Bowles. The forces arrived at the camp only to find that it had been deserted and that the Indians had retreated to the vicinity of a Delaware Indian village, where they took up a strong position in a ravine and a dense thicket. After the Indians opened fire on the volunteers, an attack was made by Colonel Burleson, Lt. Col. Deveraux J. Woodlief, and General Rusk. The attack drove the Indians from their positions. Eighteen Cherokees were found dead on the battlefield, while many of the wounded were carried away by their comrades. The Texans' losses consisted of two killed and six wounded, one mortally. According to General Douglass, the Texans captured "five kegs of powder, 250 lbs lead, many horses, and cattle, corn, and other property" including most of their baggage.[12]

On the following day, July 16, the militia began its pursuit of the Cherokees. The two regiments under Colonel Burleson and General Rusk began moving up the west bank of the Neches River. After a march of about four miles, the main force was informed by their scouts that the Indians were not far ahead of them. The Indians at first took up positions in an Indian hut and a cornfield but shortly moved to a thicket.

After heavy firing from both sides, the volunteers charged the enemy positions. The Indians broke their ranks and retreated "into a dense thicket and swamp in the Neches bottom, which was charged by the whole force." According to General Douglass, the enemy "consisted of about five hundred, their line extending at one time a mile." [13]

The Battle of the Neches was devastating to the Cherokees. At the end of a hotly contested hour and a half, there were over one hundred dead or wounded Indians on the battleground. Among those killed was Chief Bowles, the principal leader of the Cherokees. The Texan losses were only two killed, thirty wounded, three mortally.[14] Among those Texans wounded were Vice-President Burnet, General Johnston, Adjutant General Hugh McLeod, and Maj. David S. Kaufman.[15]

In their pursuit of the remaining Cherokees, the militia not only destroyed many Indian villages but also captured and scattered their livestock. General Douglass reported that the Cherokees, as well as the Delawares, Shawnees, Caddoes, Kickapoos, Biloxies, Creeks, Ouchies, Muskogees, and Seminoles, had planted extensive fields of corn, beans, and peas. A portion of these crops were destroyed by the militia in the belief that they had been planted to sustain the Indians and the Mexican troops in their war against the Texans. Douglass suggested that the government send out a force of men to destroy the remaining crops.[16] It has never been proven that the many fields of crops were going to sustain the Indians and Mexicans during a war with the Republic. Douglass estimated that there would have been enough food to supply a thousand Indians, as well as the Mexican army, for at least a year; however, the general's estimate was probably exaggerated. These tribes depended almost entirely on their crops for their annual food supply, and it is more likely that the extensive fields had been planted for their sustenance through the winter and spring.

By July 25 the pursuit of the Cherokees was halted, with scattered remnants of the Cherokees fleeing into Arkansas and other areas. After the battle on the Neches, Chief Bowles's son John became the Cherokees' leader, along with another Indian called The Egg. After remaining in hiding around the upper Trinity for several months, these chiefs began to lead the remainder of the tribe into Mexico. Their trail was discovered by Colonel Burleson and his men, and on Christmas Day of 1839 they were overtaken by the Texans near the mouth of the San Saba River. In a short but fierce fight, both John Bowles and The Egg were killed, along with five other warriors. Twenty-seven women and children were captured, including the wife of Chief Bowles and the wife, three children, and two sisters of John Bowles. All the Indians' "camp equipage," horses, and cattle were captured. The Texans lost only two men — Capt. John L. Lynch and a Tonkawa Indian. The few Indians who escaped eventually rejoined their friends in the Indian Territory.[17]

This was the last fight in which the Cherokees participated in Texas. The tribe never again presented a threat, whether real or imagined, to the settlers of Texas. With the expulsion of the Cherokees and their associated tribes, additional land was opened to the flow of Anglo settlement into the new Republic, thus ending the controversy surrounding tribal claims to Texas lands. Indian depredations in the more settled areas of the Republic became almost nonexistent. The major Indian threat was removed to the frontier areas, where settlers were daily threatened by such tribes as the Comanche and Kiowa.

☆ 3

The Council House Fight

Of all the Indian tribes within the boundaries of the Republic of Texas, the Comanches presented the most serious threat to the settlers. Regardless of numerous treaties negotiated between the Comanches and the Texans, the Brazos and Colorado river valleys continued to be plagued by Indian forays. On March 12, 1839, Lewis P. Cooke, in writing to General Johnston, had stated that he was totally "convinced that speedy relief must be had, or depopulation will necessarily soon ensue. The whole country is literally swarming with redskins." [1] The Comanches made numerous appearances in the vicinity of San Antonio in 1839 but limited their activities mostly to theft.

On January 10, 1840, Col. Henry W. Karnes, commandant of the military post at San Antonio, informed the secretary of war that three Comanche chiefs and one Mexican captive had arrived in the city the day before to discuss the possibility of a peace treaty. As evidence of their "amicable disposition," the Indians assured Colonel Karnes that their people had "refused to treat with the Cherokees, who solicited them with large presents to enter with them in a war against the Republic." They also acknowledged that the Mexican Centralists had sent emissaries to their tribe attempting to "stir up a general war with" the Texans, but these offers, too, had been rejected. The tribe informed Colonel Karnes that their nation had held a general council eighteen days earlier and had chosen a chief to discuss peace terms with the white men. Karnes refused negotiations "without the release of the American Captives, and the restoration of all stolen property; besides giving guarantees that future depredators on our property should be delivered up for punishment." [2] After informing Karnes that these stipulations would be agreeable with their council, the chiefs hastily assured him that they had had no connection with the Cherokees or the Mexican Centralists in their dealings against the Republic of Texas. They agreed to return to San Antonio in twenty or thirty days with other Comanche chiefs, as well as all their white captives, to begin peace negotiations. After being presented with gifts, which was the general custom, the Indians left the city.[3]

Distrust of the Comanches and previously broken treaties prompted the secretary of war to instruct Col. William S. Fisher, commander of the First Regiment of Infantry, to proceed immediately with three companies to San Antonio in order to seize the Indians as hostages if they failed to bring in their white prisoners as previously agreed upon. The troops would not be used if the Indians returned their captives. If the Comanches failed to fulfill their promise, they were to be held as hostages by the Texans until all the white captives were returned. Instructions were also given to dispense with the former practice of presenting gifts to the Indians. Two commissioners, Adj. Gen. Hugh McLeod and Col. William G. Cooke, were chosen to carry out the negotiations with the Indians.[4]

On the morning of March 19, two Comanche scouts arrived in San Antonio and informed the commissioners of the approaching Indians. Shortly afterwards, a party of sixty-five Indians, including men, women, and children, entered the city. With them was only one white captive, a fifteen-year-old girl named Matilda Lockhart. Following the Indians' arrival, the twelve principal chiefs were led into the Council House.

The one-story Council House was a stone building which "adjoined the stone jail on the corner of Main Plaza and Calabosa (Market) Street. The yard back of the Court House was later the City Market on Market Street." [5] This courthouse, originally constructed in the 1740s, was part of a building complex known as the Casas Reales. By 1840 these ancient buildings had undergone much reconstruction and had witnessed much history. The Casas Reales was the official residence in 1770 for Juan María Vicencio de Ripperdá. The Baron de Ripperdá was the first Spanish governor of Texas to make his headquarters in San Antonio, known at that time as San Fernando de Bexar. In 1801 the American prisoners of the Philip Nolan expedition were imprisoned in the Casas Reales. And now the old courthouse was again to play a part in the colorful history of San Antonio.[6]

Indians not involved in the peace talks inside the Council House remained outside in the courthouse yard. Here the young boys performed for the townspeople by showing off their skill at "shooting arrows at pieces of money put up by some of the Americans." [7]

Since the Indians had promised to bring in all their white captives, the Texans were somewhat surprised that only one prisoner was returned. By questioning Matilda Lockhart the commissioners learned that the Indians wanted to see if they could get a high price for her; if so, they would bring in the rest, one at a time. Matilda informed the commissioners that there were other white prisoners at the Comanches' principal camp and that she had seen them several days before.

As the council talks began, Colonel Fisher's troops were ordered into the vicinity of the council room. The Indians were then questioned as to the whereabouts of the other captives. Chief Muke-war-rah told the commissioners, "We have brought in the only one we had; the others are with other tribes." The commissioners realized this to be an outright lie. Following a pause in the council room, the chief then "asked quickly, 'How do you like answer?' " [8] Fisher responded:

> I do *not* like your answer. I told you not to come here again without bringing in your prisoners. You have come against my orders. Your women and children may depart in peace, and your braves may go and tell your people to send in the prisoners. When those prisoners are returned, your chiefs here present may likewise go free. Until then we will hold you as hostages.[9]

At this time one company of troops was marched into the council room and another one to the rear of the building. Capt. George T. Howard posted guards at the doors in the council room and lined his men across the room. The Indians were told that the soldiers were their guards and that they would not harm them if they did not resist. The chiefs, realizing their situation, strung their bows and presented their knives in preparation for a fight. Colonel Fisher ordered his troops to fire, "if they do not desist!" At that moment, one of the chiefs ran for the door and stabbed the sentinel with his knife. The Indian was ordered shot. As the chief fell dead, others attacked the soldiers, who were ordered to fire. In a matter of seconds, all twelve Comanche chiefs lay dead.[10]

Hearing the war whoops from within the Council House, the Indians in the courthouse yard realized what was happening and fled in all directions. The soldiers, firing into the crowds of people, killed both Indians and whites. The company of troops under Capt. William D. Redd, stationed in the rear of the Council House, was attacked by the Indians, who fought desperately. These Indians were forced to take shelter in the stone houses around the Council House. Another group of Indians attempted to escape across the river, but a party of mounted men under Col. Lysander Wells cut them off and killed all but one, a Mexican renegade.[11]

The Indians fled in all directions down the streets and between the houses. As the Indians were attempting to escape to the river, one was suddenly confronted by a large Negro woman who was making an attempt to protect her children as well as those of her master. As the Indian approached her, she stood bravely "with a great rock lifted in both hands above her head" crying out to the savage, "If you don't go 'way from here I'll mash your head with this rock!" The Indian, not wishing to waste his time disarming the woman, changed directions and fled down the street.[12]

Several Indians attempted to seek refuge in a stone kitchen house. Since the Indians would neither come out nor surrender, a plan was needed to force them from the building. During the night, several men got on top of the building and dropped a candlewick ball soaked in turpentine, and blaz-

ing, through a hole in the roof upon one Indian's head and
so hurt and frightened them both that they opened the door
and rushed out — to their deaths.[13]

(In the short but fierce battle, out of a total of sixty-five
Indians, sixty-four were either killed or taken prisoner. Only
one renegade Mexican escaped. Thirty chiefs and warriors,
three women, and two children were killed. Twenty-seven
women and children and two old men were locked in the city
jail. In addition to the captives taken, over one hundred
horses and many buffalo robes and peltries were confiscated.[14]
Even though the Indians were greatly outnumbered and
were required to fight with primitive weapons such as bows,
arrows, and knives, they were able to inflict casualties on the
Texans because of the ferocity of their attack.) The Texans'
losses were as follows:

> Killed — Lieut. W. M. Dunnington, First Infantry;
> private [Frederick] Kaminski, of (A) company; private
> [Robert J.] Whitney, of (E) company; Judge Thompson, of
> Houston; Judge [Julian] Hood, of Bexar; Mr. Casey [G. W.
> Cayce], of Matagorda county, and a Mexican, name un-
> known. Total killed, seven.
> List of Wounded — Capt. George T. Howard, Capt.
> Mathew Caldwell, Lieut. Edward A. Thompson, First In-
> fantry; private [Martin] Kelly, company (I); Judge Robin-
> son; Mr. Higginbotham; Mr. Morgan, and Mr. Carson.
> Total wounded, eight.[15]

The Texans entered a twelve-day truce with the Indians
in which they would be able to exchange the Indians captured
at the Council House Fight for the white prisoners at the Comanche village. One Indian squaw was released, given provi-
sions and a horse, and was permitted to go to the Comanche
camp to take the news of the Indians' defeat and prepare for
an exchange of prisoners.

On April 3, Chief Piava and a squaw arrived in San Antonio and announced that the Comanches had brought in
white captives for exchange. The chief was presented gifts of
"bread, brown sugar candy cones (peloncillo) and a beef."
The talks resumed on April 4. Although the consultation "almost reached blows" at times because of the tension and

harsh feelings, a total of seven captives were finally returned
to the Texans. One of these was a boy, Booker L. Webster.[16]
He related that when the Comanches heard about the deaths
of their chiefs in San Antonio they

> howled and cut themselves with knives, and killed horses,
> for several days. And they took all the American captives,
> thirteen in number, and roasted and butchered them to
> death with horrible cruelties; that he and a little girl named
> Putnam, five years old, had been spared because they had
> previously been adopted into the tribe.[17]

Evidence that the Comanches had treated their prisoners
cruelly is found in the examples of the conditions of the Putnam girl and Matilda Lockhart. When Matilda Lockhart arrived in San Antonio with the Comanches, she was being used
as a herder for the Indians' extra ponies. There were many
bruises and sores on her head, arms, and face, and her nose
was "actually burnt off to the bone — all the fleshy end gone,
and a great scab formed on the end of the bone. Both nostrils
were wide open and denuded of flesh." The girl related how
the Indians beat her and woke her in the night by "sticking a
chunk of fire to her flesh." [18] The Putnam girl was in much
the same condition.

The Indians who had been made prisoners at the Council
House Fight were later moved from the city jail to the San
José Mission; from there they were removed to Camp Cooke
at the head of the San Antonio River. Lax security helped
them to gradually escape and return to their own people.
None of these prisoners were treated unkindly, but they never
trusted the kindness that was offered them. Several were actually taken into people's homes to live and work, but they ran
away when opportunities arose.[19]

The Comanches remained in the vicinity of San Antonio
for the rest of the spring and part of the summer while recover-
ing from the severe defeat which had been dealt to them at the
Council House Fight. Small parties of Comanches continued
stealing livestock, burning houses, and attacking individual
settlers. However, the death of twelve of their chiefs was a serious blow to the Comanches, and they finally retired to Comanchería among the hills above San Antonio and Austin to
make preparations to strike back at the Texans.

☆ 4

Comanche Raids on Victoria and Linnville

Late in May of 1840 the Texas government received word that General Canalizo, in Matamoros, was once again attempting to incite the Indians to wage war upon the white settlers. Hoping to take advantage of the Indian situation following the expulsion of the Cherokees, the killing of Chief Bowles, and the greatest outrage — the slaughter of the Comanche chiefs at the Council House in San Antonio — Canalizo once again sent Mexican emissaries into Texas to visit the Indians, primarily the Comanches. As soon as the news was confirmed that an Indian raid was imminent, Dr. Branch T. Archer, the secretary of war for the Republic, called for the formation of additional militia companies to repel the Indians. The attack never came, and after several weeks the volunteers dispersed and returned to their homes. It is almost certain that Mexican spies had been stationed in Texas to observe the movements of the Texans and that the Indian raid was delayed because of the precautionary measures taken by the Texans. Shortly after the dispersal of the volunteers, the Comanches began their Great Comanche Raid of 1840.[1]

The Indian raid, which caught the Texans unaware, caused the deaths of many settlers and the destruction of much property. To understand how the Indians could make a

surprise attack on Victoria and Linnville, so far from their villages, it is necessary to have some knowledge about the geog-
raphy of the region at that time. One author describes it as follows:

> At the time of this raid the country between the Guadalupe
> and San Marcos, on the west, and the Colorado on the east,
> above a line drawn from Gonzales to La Grange, was a wil-
> derness, while below that line it was thinly settled. Between
> Gonzales and Austin, on Plum Creek, were two recent set-
> tlers, Isom J. Goode and John A. Neill. From Gonzales to
> within a few miles of La Grange there was not a settler.
> There was not one between Gonzales and Bastrop, nor one
> between Austin and San Antonio. A road from Gonzales to
> Austin, then in the first year of its existence, had been
> opened in July 1839.[2]

With little effort, then, the war party of Indians was able
to move down through Central Texas virtually unnoticed.
Seething over their losses at the Council House Fight, the Comanches had been agitated by Mexican agents to make war
on the Texans. During the night of August 4, a war party of
approximately 600 Comanche and Kiowa Indians, accompanied by a few Mexicans, descended from the Hill Country
above San Antonio, San Marcos, and Austin and began their
march to the coast in an effort to avenge the deaths of their
chiefs.[3]

The first Texan encounter with the Indians occurred on
August 5 in the Hallettsville area.[4] Dr. Joel Ponton and
Tucker Foley, en route from Columbus to Gonzales, came
upon a group of twenty-seven Indians from the main war
party. Immediately upon seeing the Indians, the two men
turned their horses and attempted to outrun the Comanches
to a creek three miles behind them. Dr. Ponton, who was riding a slow horse, was soon overtaken. However, it became evident that the Indians were more interested in capturing the
faster horse ridden by Tucker Foley. As the Indians overtook
Ponton they attempted to make a passing attack on his life.
Having received several wounds, Ponton fell from his horse
and pretended to be dead. After the Indians had all disappeared, he crawled into a thicket and some tall grass and hid
there.

Following a three-mile chase, Foley reached Ponton Creek, where he tried to hide in the water but was soon discovered and captured. The Indians then returned to where Ponton had been left for dead. Unable to locate him, the Indians made Foley call for his companion, who, of course, refused to answer. The Comanches then tortured Foley by cutting off the bottoms of his feet and forcing him to walk some distance. The Indians then shot and scalped him.[5]

During the night, Dr. Ponton made his way to his home in the Lavaca settlement and related the attack made upon himself and Tucker Foley. Immediately, Capt. Adam Zumwalt and thirty-six men set out for the scene of the attack. After locating Foley's body and burying him, the men began their pursuit of the Indians.[6] On that same day a mail carrier from Austin arrived in Gonzales and reported the discovery of a large, fresh Indian trail crossing Plum Creek and leading southward. A group of twenty-four men was then assembled by Capt. Ben McCulloch and hastened to the Big Hill area, where they hoped to locate the Indian trail.[7] They set up camp for the night at the Big Hill, also known as McClure's Hill. Early on the morning of August 7, the trail was located. During the morning, Captain Zumwalt's men from the Lavaca settlement joined McCulloch's force and the combined parties began following the trail. About midday the forces, consisting of sixty men, noticed a group of approaching horsemen. The third party of men constituted "a company of sixty-five men from Victoria and the Quero *sic* or Blair's settlement, under the command of Captain John T[u]mlinson." [8] With the combined forces, numbering 125, the men continued their pursuit in a "brisk trot." After combining forces with Captain Tumlinson, they learned that the Indians had attacked the town of Victoria. Only after the Indians had retired for the night were Tumlinson's men able to go for help from neighboring settlements.[9]

At 4:00 P.M. on August 6, the Comanche war party made its sudden appearance on the northern outskirts of Victoria, sweeping down from the direction of Spring Creek. The citizens were caught completely unprepared, since they had not been informed of any hostile Indians in the vicinity.[10] When the Indians first appeared, the citizens of the town thought that they were a group of Lipans, a tribe that was friendly toward the settlers and that frequently visited Victoria to trade with the white man.[11] It was not until the war party had surrounded the town and begun riding in toward the citizens and yelling loudly that the people realized what was happening. No concentration of defense could be made because the Indians were everywhere around the edges of the town. Few arms could be obtained on such short notice, but the people were able to prevent the Comanches from entering the populated sections of town. One group of citizens made an unprepared charge upon the Indians, which resulted in the deaths of Dr. Arthur Gray and William McMin Nuner and the wounding of several other men. In many parts of the town the Indians were repulsed and were forced to remain on the outskirts.[12]

In this raid on Victoria many of the Indians collected and drove away all the cattle and horses they could find. Several Mexican traders who were visiting Victoria at the time had over 500 head of horses staked on the prairie surrounding the town. The Comanches took all these horses as well as many others found running loose.[13] A large number of horses owned by "Scotch" Sutherland and recently brought to Victoria were also captured by the Indians, bringing their total capture count to approximately 1,500 horses and mules.[14]

Late in the afternoon, the Comanches retired to Spring Creek, three miles from Victoria. While near Spring Creek, the Indians killed a settler named Varlan Richeson and two Negro men, and they captured a Negro girl. During the night, a group of men from Victoria left the town in search of reinforcements. These men passed near the Indians' camp on their way to the Cuero settlement in De Witt County.[15]

When making raids on the settlers, it was the usual custom of the Comanches to gather their plunder and then retire to their homes before the Texans were able to assemble a force to attack them. However, contrary to custom, the Indians once again surrounded and attacked Victoria on the morning of August 7. A party of men returning from Jackson County encountered the Indians about a mile from Victoria. Pinckney Caldwell and a Mexican man were killed by the Indians, while the other two men in the party, Joseph Rodgers and Jesse O. Wheeler, rushed into the town with the enemy close behind. The Indians succeeded in burning one house and robbing several others near the edge of town, but after meeting strong resistance from the citizens of the town they decided to move in the direction of the lower settlements, herding up livestock as they proceeded toward the coast.[16]

The Indians continued down the country to near Nine Mile Point, where they captured Mrs. Cyrus Crosby (granddaughter of the famous pioneer Daniel Boone) and her child.[17] (The Comanches then began moving eastward in the direction of Linnville.) Nine miles from Victoria the Indians attacked the Van Norman ranch and from there proceeded to the Clausel ranch, located nine miles from Linnville. The Indians wounded Mr. Clausel, burned his house, and stole many of his cattle and horses.[18]

On the night of August 7 the Indians established their camp along Placedo Creek, on the Benavides ranch, twelve miles from Linnville. While there, the Indians killed a wagoner named Stephens. Another man, a Frenchman, escaped from the Indians by hiding in the thick foliage and moss of a large oak tree.[19]

During the night William G. Ewing, a merchant traveling from Linnville to Victoria, noticed Stephens's empty wagon and a great number of campfires along the creek. Thinking the camp to be that of Mexican traders bound for Linnville, Ewing passed near there and proceeded to Victoria, where he learned of the Indian raid. The man became very distraught when he learned how close he had been to the Indians' camp.[20]

On the morning of August 8 the Indians again moved in the direction of Linnville. Along the way Mrs. Crosby's small child, being hungry and tired, began to cry. The mother was unable to quiet the child, and one of the Indians "snatched the babe from her, cast it upon the ground and speared it before her eyes."[21]

Shortly after Mrs. Crosby's child was killed, the Indians made their appearance at about 8:00 A.M. on the Victoria road. Several of the citizens of Linnville discovered the Indi-

ans about two miles from town.[22] Being unaware of any large
Indian war party in the area, the citizens supposed the Indians to be Mexican traders bringing in a large *caballado* of
horses to sell or trade. The citizens of Linnville did not become aware of the impending danger until the Indians "approached near to the town, which they did riding nearly at full
speed, and in the shape of a half moon for the purpose of surrounding the town." As they approached, the Indians killed
two Negro slaves owned by Maj. Hugh O. Watts. They also
killed a white man named Joseph O'Neill.[23]

As the Comanches launched their savage assault upon
the coastal town of Linnville, the bewildered inhabitants,
many of whom were without guns or any form of defense,
began to retreat and tried to reach safety on boats anchored in
the bay. Many found refuge on the steamer *Mustang*, which
was lying offshore. The Comanches pursued the fleeing inhabitants into the water. In attempting to reach safety Major
Watts, the customs collector for the port of Linnville, was
killed; his wife and a Negro woman and child were overtaken
and made captives. A number of accounts of the burning of
Linnville indicate that Major Watts and his recently married
wife had reached safety but had returned to shore to recover a
gold watch that had been left behind, only to be overtaken by
the Indians.[24]

As the inhabitants watched from their boats, the Comanches burned, looted, and destroyed the town. Judge John
Hays became "exasperated" at the sight and "vowed he
would have one shot at the 'red devils' anyway." Without hes-
itating, the judge grabbed a gun and leaped into the bay. The
water was three or four feet deep, and he waded to the shore,
where he shouted at the savages and threatened them to come
within range of his gun. The Indians, thinking this man to be
"bad medicine," cautiously avoided him. After much persua-
sion from his friends, the judge returned to the boat. Every-
one, including the judge, was surprised when his gun was ex-
amined and found to be unloaded.[25]

The Indians spent the entire day in the town plundering
and burning its many stores and houses. Feather beds were
dragged from many of the houses and tied to the tails of the

horses. Holes were cut in the ticking, and the Indians would yell in amusement as the feathers went flying. The Indians also seemed to find great enjoyment in tying lengthy bolts of cloth to their horses' tails and racing through the burning town. The inhabitants watched helplessly from their boats as almost all the buildings in Linnville were burned and destroyed. Large numbers of cattle were herded into pens, where they were burned or cut to pieces by the savages. Almost everything of value was either taken or destroyed by the Indians.[26]

Linnville had been established as an important shipping point on the Gulf Coast, and consequently many warehouses in the town were filled with all kinds of merchandise. In one warehouse owned by John J. Linn the Indians found several cases of hats and umbrellas. This merchandise belonged to James Robinson, a merchant from San Antonio, and was going to be shipped overland to him. The Indians, wearing the hats and waving the umbrellas, went racing up and down the streets between the burning buildings.[27] Included in the diversity of plunder taken by the Indians were fine clothes, ribbons, and bolts of cloth. Walter P. Webb writes:

> The warriors put on the coats, the chiefs the tall hats, and they plaited the bright ribbons and calicoes from the warehouses into their horses' manes and tails, making gay streamers as the riders dashed about in the stiff sea breeze of the coast.[28]

The Indians began to retire late in the afternoon, carrying with them several hundred horses and mules loaded with the plunder taken from the stores and warehouses of Linnville. With the town in flames, they withdrew across a nearby bayou and established their camp for the night. There they planned to begin their return trip with their immense plunder to their homeland in the Hill Country to the northwest.

While Linnville was being burned, other Texans were making preparations to intercept the Indians. Captain Tumlinson and his party of 125 men left Victoria and moved eastward on the Texana road. They established a camp about midnight at the Casa Blanca water hole and later sent a messenger (George Kerr) to Texana for reinforcements. At about

eleven the next morning the Indian war party was discovered
on the west bank of Garcitas Creek, near its junction with Ar-
enosa Creek. Captain Tumlinson's right flankers, being more
than a mile away from the main force and unaware of the Indians, were cut off and unable to rejoin Tumlinson's volunteers. The Texans began to advance upon the Indians in par-
allel divisions. The Gonzales and Lavaca companies occupied
the right nearest the Indians, while the Victoria and Cuero
companies were to the left about twenty paces. The Indians,
"sporting huge helmets of buffalo or elk-horns — armed with
glistening shields, with bows and quivers, with guns and
lances, and mounted on fleet chargers," began to prepare for
the Texans' advance.[29] When they got close to the Indians,
Captain Tumlinson's volunteers dismounted in the open prairie. The Indians began to encircle the Texans in their customary manner of warfare. While a portion of the war party occupied Tumlinson and his men, the rest of the Indians ran
with their pack animals and plunder to safety. The Indians,
who greatly outnumbered the Texans, seemed to be more con-
cerned with the safety of their booty than with killing the Texans. A fifteen- or twenty-minute skirmish ensued in which one
man, Benjamin Mordecai of Victoria, was killed. After losing
several warriors the Indians began a hasty retreat, with Tumlinson's men in close pursuit.[30]

On August 10 Captain Tumlinson was joined by Capt.
Clarke Owen and forty men from Texana. Owen reported
having a minor skirmish with the Indians the day before. In
this fight one man — a Dr. Bell — was lost. Having extra
horses that were stolen from Victoria and Linnville, the Indians were able to change mounts in order to gain distance on
the Texans who had no fresh mounts. After following the Indians for twenty miles without a fight, Ben McCulloch, along
with Alsey S. Miller, Archibald Gipson, and Barney Randell,
gave up the chase. They decided to leave the group, circle
around the Indians by way of Gonzales, and assemble a force
at Plum Creek to defeat the raiding Comanches.[31] Consequently, this action enabled these four men to take part in the
Battle of Plum Creek, while Tumlinson's men were too late,
reaching the battlefield several hours after the fight.

While the Indians were among the lower settlements and were plundering and devastating the countryside, a series of movements occurred which culminated in their defeat on Plum Creek near Lockhart. By August 7 news of the raid on Victoria had reached the Lavaca settlement. Lafayette Ward and twenty-two volunteers immediately left the home of James Kerr on the Lavaca River and proceeded to the Big Hill area, where they hoped to locate the Indians' trail. Unable to find the trail, the men concluded that the Indians were returning on the west side of the Guadalupe River. The Lavaca volunteers then continued on to Gonzales, where they joined up with the famous Texas Indian fighter, Mathew "Old Paint" Caldwell.[32] Caldwell agreed that the Indians would recross the Guadalupe near the present site of New Braunfels. The Lavaca volunteers, joined by Caldwell and thirty-nine followers, proceeded on to Seguin. After a hard ride, the men reached Seguin on the morning of August 10. While there they were overtaken by a messenger from Gonzales who informed the group that the Indians were retreating on their downward made trail. It was then realized that the Indians must be met on Plum Creek. By nightfall the men made their camp at the San Antonio crossing of the San Marcos River. The temperature the following day was extremely hot, and across the burnt prairie to Plum Creek dust and flying ashes were blinding and stifling to both men and horses. By evening the companies under Ward and Caldwell had reached Isham Good's cabin on the Gonzales-Austin road.[33] At about the same time, Maj. Gen. Felix Huston, commander of the Texas Militia, and his aide, James Izod, arrived from Austin. The force of men proceeded to Plum Creek, approximately three miles west of Good's cabin. At the creek they found Capt. James Bird and thirty men from Gonzales. They set up camp and posted sentries to watch for the approaching Indians.[34]

News of the raids on Victoria and Linnville was spread throughout the country. Following their departure from Tumlinson's group on August 10, Ben McCulloch and his three companions arrived in Gonzales soliciting the aid of those who would help defeat the Indians. McCulloch immediately sent Alsey Miller in search of Captain Caldwell, while he and

Capt. James Bird engaged in forming a "minute company" made up of citizens of Gonzales. Henry McCulloch was sent to the Big Hill area east of Gonzales for the purpose of reporting the enemy's advancement. He subsequently reported that the Indians had passed within several yards of where he had been hiding, and he had seen Tumlinson's men in pursuit.

Ben McCulloch dispatched Archibald Gipson with a message to Col. Edward Burleson on the Colorado River.[35] The message notified Burleson of the raids on Victoria and Linnville and informed him that the Texans hoped to intercept the Indians and defeat them before they were able to escape to the Hill Country above San Marcos. Because of the urgency of the message Burleson and a friend, the Reverend Z. N. Morrell, immediately went up the Colorado River Valley to Bastrop, informing settlers of the news and gathering volunteers along the way. Good's Crossing on Plum Creek was agreed upon as the spot where the Indians would be intercepted. An express rider and Reverend Morrell were sent to Austin to spread the news and call for volunteers to help in the defeat of the Indians. Morrell returned to Bastrop thirty minutes after Colonel Burleson's group left for Plum Creek. After a hard ride, Morrell overtook Burleson and arrived on Plum Creek just in time to participate in the battle.[36]

Colonel Burleson's group consisted of eighty-seven volunteers, mostly from the Bastrop area, and thirteen Tonkawa Indians led by their chief Placido. The Tonkawas did not have horses and were compelled to travel on foot. Runners kept Burleson informed as to the events taking place at Plum Creek. In order to reach Plum Creek in time to participate in the battle, Burleson's men had to advance at a gallop for the last three or four miles. The Tonkawas, who were horseless, kept up with the mounted volunteers and also arrived in time to participate in the fight against their inveterate enemies — the Comanches.[37]

By the early morning of August 12, 1840, the number of Texas volunteers at Good's Crossing on Plum Creek had steadily grown. The combined force commanded by Caldwell and Ward consisted of sixty-three men; the group of Gonzales volunteers led by Capt. James Bird numbered thirty. The force also included Ben McCulloch and three companions; Maj. Gen. Felix Huston, accompanied by his aide, Major Izod; and Isham Good, who lived in the vicinity. Just prior to the battle, Colonel Burleson arrived with his eighty-seven volunteers and thirteen Tonkawa Indians, building the volunteer militia up to two hundred. Thus the stage was set for the destruction of the Comanches at Plum Creek.

Interception @ Plum Creek
no volunteer militia

☆ 5

The Battle of Plum Creek

At Captain Caldwell's request several scouts were dispatched to observe the Indians and report their progress. On August 12, at about daylight, Robert Hall and John Baker reported sighting the Indians several miles down the creek and moving toward the Texans' encampment. In less than twenty minutes, the men were mounted and prepared for the imminent fight. A leader was needed to command the combined militias, and immediately the volunteers turned to the man with the most experience at fighting Indians: Capt. Mathew Caldwell. The captain first posed a question to the men. "Boys, there are eight hundred or one thousand Indians — they have our women and children prisoners — they have repulsed our men below — we are eighty-seven strong, and I believe can whip h–ll out of 'em! Boys, shall we fight?"

Following a rousing reply, Caldwell asked that the command be given to Major General Huston. "Boys, gratify me by voting aye!" The men reluctantly voted on Huston as their commander. Out of respect for Huston's position as major general of the Texas army, no one voted against him, although most of the men would have preferred Caldwell.[1]

Immediately the Texan force "crossed above the Indian trail about three miles, and passed down on the west side."

After following the creek through a wooded area, the men crossed several ravines and emerged into a small open glade which was separated and concealed from the rest of the large open prairie by dense timber. At this point the men were overtaken by Owen Hardeman and Hutchinson Reed from Bastrop. These scouts informed Huston that Colonel Burleson and his men were within a few miles and were advancing hurriedly in order to take part in the fight. Because of their pressing need for reinforcements, Huston's troops halted their advancement and awaited Burleson's arrival. Huston then announced his plan of attack. His strategy called for a "hollow square, open in front." The right line would be commanded by Colonel Burleson, while the left line would be commanded by Captain Caldwell. The rear line, or reserve, would be made up of Bird's and Ward's companies commanded by Maj. Thomas Monroe Hardeman.[2]

As the Texans lay concealed and awaited Colonel Burleson's arrival, the Indians came into full view. Unaware of the Texans, they proceeded to move diagonally across the open prairie. The Indian procession consisted of warriors, their squaws and children, older men and women of the tribe, and a large *caballado* of approximately two thousand to three thousand stolen horses and mules, many laden with plunder taken from Victoria and Linnville. The entire cavalcade, stretching for several miles across the prairie, posed an awesome spectacle as it moved across the open country. The Indian warriors created a most impressive appearance as they rode about, singing and gyrating in various ways. From the Indians and their horses were tied "fluttering ribbons streaming in the breeze, and other gaudy appendages of savage finery."[3]

The Comanche warriors, having combined the white man's garments with their customary apparel, presented a rather grotesque appearance.

> There was a huge warrior, who wore a stovepipe hat, and another one who wore a fine pigeon-tailed cloth coat, buttoned up *behind*. They seemed to have a talent for finding and blending the strangest, most unheard-of ornaments. Some wore on their heads immense buck and buffalo horns. One headdress . . . consisted of a large white crane with red eyes.[4]

Following the sacking and burning of Linnville, many of the Comanche warriors clothed themselves in the white man's attire they had found in the stores and warehouses of the port town. When the Indians appeared at Plum Creek, one chief, in particular, caught the Texans' attention:

> He was riding a very fine horse, held in by a fine American bridle, with a red ribbon eight or ten feet long, tied to the tail of the horse. He was dressed in elegant style from the goods stolen at Linnville, with a high top silk hat, fine pair of boots and leather gloves, an elegant broadcloth coat hind part before, with brass buttons shining brightly right up and down his back. When first he made his appearance, he was carrying a large umbrella stretched.[5]

While Huston's forces had awaited Burleson's arrival, the Indians had moved across the prairie and were about a mile and a half ahead of the Texans. As Burleson's men arrived at Plum Creek, a "whispered cheer" arose from the volunteers. Burleson quickly replied, "Howdy, boys! no time for cheers now. Men, fall into line and form the right wing." [6]

Four Texans were immediately dispatched to spy on the Indians. As the men approached the savages, the rear guard of the war party turned back to meet the spies. When the Indians were within close range, Dr. Alonzo B. Sweitzer fired his gun, killing one. The other three Indians that composed the rear guard turned and fled into the main body of the war party.[7] Hearing Sweitzer's shot, Burleson's men began to proceed at full speed. As the men came within sight of the Indians, they were puzzled to see confusion among the Indians' ranks. It appeared that a group of white men was being chased by a portion of the war party.[8] Later it was discovered that a squad of volunteers, not associated with Huston's command, accidentally came upon the Indians' advanced guard. Thinking that they could defeat such a small band of Indians, they dismounted and secured positions in a live oak grove. When the men saw the main war party behind the advanced guard, they mounted their horses and retreated. In haste, one of the men was left by his horse as well as by his companions. The Indians bore down upon him and killed him.[9]

As soon as the Texans came onto the open prairie, they

were spotted by the Indians. The Comanches immediately formed a line of defense between the Texans and their stolen horses and plunder. The Indians then pressed onward in a northwesterly direction toward the safety of their camps, and stragglers, bringing up the rear, engaged in minor skirmishing with the Texans for about five miles across the prairie. With the Texan forces continuing to draw closer to the main body of the war party, the Comanches halted their retreat at a place later known as Kelley Springs.[10] Most of the warriors "took position in a point of oaks on the left, with the Clear Fork in their rear, and a small boggy branch on their left, but in the line of their retreat." [11] There they awaited the Texans' attack. The volunteers advanced to within 150 yards when Huston ordered a halt. Orders were then given to dismount and form the "hollow square" formation agreed upon. Many of the Indian fighters were astonished at the order to dismount. They had hoped to charge into the midst of the Indians. While the Texans formed their lines, about twenty or thirty Comanche warriors and chiefs began encircling the volunteers, firing at them from a distance of sixty to eighty yards.[12]

As the warriors circled the Texans, the women and old men of the tribe used the time to drive all their horses and pack animals toward safety. (The Indians continued to charge the Texans for about thirty minutes.) The Texans finally realized that one of the prominent chiefs, who had been charging very close to the Texans' position, wore a shield which protected him from the white man's bullets. They noticed that every time the chief would come to an abrupt halt and turn his horse, the shield would fly up, thus exposing his body. When the chief once again charged the Texans, several volunteers fired as the Indian's shield flew up. The chief fell to the ground. Several other warriors lost their lives in attempting to recover his body, but the Indians kept trying until the chief was removed from the battlefield.[13] Having carried the chief to the point of oaks where the concentration of Comanches was centered, the Indians began howling strangely. Captain Caldwell, realizing the time was right for a charge, said to Major General Huston, "Now, General, is your time to charge them! They are whipped." [14] Ben McCulloch, also impatient to charge, pleaded with Huston:

General Huston, this is no way to fight Indians; they
are fooling with us. They are running off with their captives
and plunder — order a charge, and we can kill hundreds,
and rescue the women and children.

All right, Ben, a charge it is then! Mount and charge.[15]

Observing that a major concentration of Indians was assembled in a particular wooded area, Huston "ordered Colonel Burleson with the right wing to move around the point of
woods, and Captain Caldwell with the left wing to charge into
the woods, which movements were executed in gallant style."
Unable to withstand the Texans' assault, the main portion of
the war party was dispersed. The Indians broke into small
parties and began a hasty retreat, fighting along the way.[16]

In their retreat the Indians came to a boggy branch
which they were compelled to cross. The speed of their retreat
was greatly reduced as they began to cross the morass, and
several Indians were overtaken and killed by the Texans.
Large numbers of pack animals, being so burdened with plunder, bogged down in the swamp area. (Many of the pack
mules carried heavy "hoop-irons" to be used in making arrow
points.) The pack animals were so numerous that a person
"could have walked along on their bodies *dry*." After crossing
the boggy branch, officers made no attempt to command the
Texan forces. The small groups of Indians ran toward the hills
above San Marcos, while the volunteers pursued them for approximately twelve to fifteen miles. The pursuit was ended between the present-day towns of San Marcos and Kyle.[17]

Many incidents illustrating details of the fight and individual heroism occurred during the Battle of Plum Creek. The
close individual combat in which many of the Texans and Indians were engaged during the battle was exemplified in a
death struggle between Alsey Miller and one of the Comanche
warriors. While in pursuit of several Indians, Miller raised his
rifle to fire; however, the gun misfired and one of the braves,
seizing the opportunity, turned and rushed Miller. The rifle
that Miller had carried with him into battle was an old-fash-
ioned, seven-shot repeating rifle with a large brass cylinder
that had to be revolved by hand each time it was fired. In his
haste Miller failed to turn the cylinder far enough to catch,

and before he could correct the situation, the Indian was upon him. As the two men passed on horseback the Indian had already adjusted an arrow and was drawing back on his bow when Miller quickly raised his gun and struck the Indian on the side of his head, causing him to drop his bow. The brave immediately grabbed a handful of arrows from his quiver and attempted to stab Miller. As Miller eluded the Indian's thrusts, he calmly corrected the problem with his gun and shot the Indian.[18]

At the time of the battle Ben McCulloch and Dr. Sweitzer were known to be great enemies. During the fight, McCulloch was in the act of reloading his gun when an Indian attempted to kill him. Dr. Sweitzer, realizing McCulloch's situation, immediately shot the Indian. McCulloch never once turned around to thank Sweitzer, but he was able to repay the doctor by saving his life in a similar situation moments later. During the fight neither man spoke to the other.[19]

In their pursuit of the Indians, the Texans saw fifteen of them fleeing up a hill in the distance. Behind the group was a lone rider chasing after them. From the appearance of his hat and the color of his horse, many of the men thought the rider was Ben McCulloch. The Texans began to cheer, "Look at Ben McCulloch, he is running a whole gang of them! Hurrah for Ben!" The men were somewhat astonished to see the rider overtake the band of Comanches and proceed on with them. They then realized that they had been cheering an Indian who was riding a horse and wearing a hat like that of McCulloch.[20]

During the running fight, one of the Indian warriors had his horse shot out from under him. He continued on foot for a short distance but then stopped and returned to his dead horse. Andrew Sowell shot at the warrior, but his bullet struck the Indian's shield. The Comanche grabbed the bridle from his horse and turned to run, but another Texan, with a loaded gun, hastened to the scene and killed the Indian. The warrior had lost his life in an attempt to regain a bridle worth less than two dollars.[21]

One of the most unusual incidents to occur during the fight was related in the death of a particular Comanche chief. After the old chief's head appeared to have been "nearly

blown off," all the Texans' efforts to knock the chief from his
horse proved futile. The Indian, stiff and rigid and clinging to
his saddlehorn, dashed about the battlefield. A great number
of the Texans claimed to have "struck him on the head with
the butt of their muskets as they passed him," but none were
able to knock the chief from his horse. The horse ran into the
woods and the chief was never found.[22]

The thirteen Tonkawa Indians who had accompanied
Burleson's men to Plum Creek exhibited heroic courage and
action throughout the fight. Although they were without
horses prior to the battle, it was only a short while before the
Tonkawas were all mounted upon horses acquired from Comanches whom they had slain. Seemingly unaware of any
danger, the Tonkawas would dart among the Comanche warriors. Placido, the Tonkawa chief, and his braves wore white
rags tied to their arms so the Texans would not mistake them
for the enemy.[23]

Seven Texans were wounded in the fight with the Comanches. One of the men received a very peculiar wound.
While in the act of shooting an Indian, James Nichols was
shot between the forefinger and middle finger. The musket
ball lodged in his right wrist, where it remained for the rest of
his life. As the wound healed, "the two fingers grew together
up to the first joint." Samuel Hutchinson Reed was also
wounded as he charged an Indian. Reed pulled the trigger but
his gun did not fire. The Indian shot an arrow which entered
below the shoulder blade, pierced Reed's lungs, and "lodged
against his right breastbone to the depth of about nine
inches." In the early moments of the battle Robert Hall received a wound in the thigh. The wound bled so profusely that
the blood "sloshed out" of his boot.[24]

During the wild confusion of retreat, the Comanches endeavored to kill their captives taken in the raids upon Victoria
and Linnville. As the Indians began their retreat, Mrs.
Crosby, who had been captured near Victoria, dismounted
and made an effort to escape into a thicket. In her attempt she
was killed by a Comanche warrior who shot two arrows which
"passed clear through her." Not far from Mrs. Crosby were
found a large Negro woman and her child hiding in the grass.

When discovered by Robert Hall, the Negro woman cried, "Bless God, here is a white man once more." [25]

At the beginning of the retreat a woman's screams attracted the attention of Reverend Morrell. Rushing into the woods, Morrell found Mrs. Watts, whose husband had been killed in Linnville, with an arrow lodged in her breast. The woman was trying to remove the arrow but was unable to dislodge the shaft. Reverend Morrell was at first unable to remove the arrow because the woman refused to release her hold on the shaft — she could not stand the pain. Dr. David F. Brown of Bastrop was summoned to the scene and, with Reverend Morrell holding the woman's hands to her sides, Dr. Brown attempted to extract the arrow. The woman "screamed so violently that he desisted." The doctor's second attempt was successful and the arrow was withdrawn. After having the arrow removed, Mrs. Watts rested upon Reverend Morrell's blanket, using his saddle as a pillow. She would doubtlessly have been killed had not the steel corset which she wore deflected the warrior's arrow.[26] Having rested for a while, she then asked for Mrs. Crosby, not knowing of her fate. She related how "the Indians whipped the poor woman frequently and called her a 'peon,' because she could not read." Mrs. Watts had been forced to ride a pack mule all the way from the coast, and at night, along the trail, the Indians gathered around her and asked her to read to them and explain the pictures in books they had stolen. (Sometimes the Indians had other uses for the books: It is said that they would tie the books to their saddles and would tear out pages for rolling cigarettes.) [27]

At the beginning of the Texans' attack many of the Indians' pack animals stampeded across the open prairies and into the wooded areas. Some of these were overtaken and recovered by the Texans. On reaching the boggy branch, many of the horses and mules became caught in the swampy area and were abandoned by the Indians. The Texans recovered a large part of the Indian pack train, but many of the pack animals were never found.

The Indians had taken a great variety of plunder in their raids on Victoria and, especially, Linnville. Among the arti-

cles found by the Texans were tobacco, black silk, calico
sheeting, clothes, eating utensils, and books. A shipment of
whiskey and brandy "to be used on surveying expeditions"
had been taken by the Indians, but there is no report of this
shipment ever being recovered.[28] Other unusual items found
in the possession of the Indians were "large portions of human
flesh, evidently prepared for cooking" and baby alligators
packed in the Indians' bundles. Some of the men thought the
Comanches were carrying the alligators back as curiosities;
others believed that by returning with the alligators the Indians could "prove to the rest of the tribe that they had gone
down as far as the coast." [29]

When the battle was over, the Texans gathered up the
immense spoils left on the battlefield by the Comanches.
Identified articles were, in every case, returned to their own-
ers, but much of the plunder could not be identified and was
divided among the men who took part in the fight. John Jenkins received, among other things, a Comanche mule with red
ribbons tied to its ears and tail. Robert Hall received a pack
mule carrying "a pillow and a bolster of homemade cloth and
considerable dry goods. There were also coverlets, sheets,
quilts, and clothing." [30]

Not all the goods stolen by the Indians were recovered.
In addition to pack animals stampeding into oblivion, the Indians, burdened by the weight of their plunder, began to
lighten their loads for an easier escape. Many of the warriors
concealed stolen articles in thickets or hastily buried their
plunder. In one instance, several slave girls who were tending
their master's cattle saw a band of Indians approaching very
fast. The young girls hid themselves and watched the Indians
spread a large blanket upon the ground. The Indians placed
several unidentifiable articles on the blanket and then, using
their knives, quickly scraped a small amount of dirt over the
blanket. The Indians then continued their hasty retreat.
Within a few moments a group of white men appeared and
rode after them. The frightened girls ran to their master's
house to report their observations; however, they had been so
scared that they were never able to relocate the spot on which
the Indians had buried their "valuables." [31]

When the Texans ended their twelve- to fifteen-mile pursuit, they returned to where the initial attack had been made earlier in the day. There they found the body of Mrs. Crosby and buried her under a large oak tree near the battlefield.[32] Through the efforts and donations made by the Lockhart Masonic Lodge, the remains of Mrs. Crosby were reinterred in 1850, ten years after the battle. There is no available information as to where the second burial took place.[33]

After returning to the battlefield where the fight had begun, the Texans were joined by volunteer forces which had arrived too late to take an active part in the battle. Col. John H. Moore had come from Fayette County with a group of men; Captain Tumlinson, Adam Zumwalt, and Clarke L. Owen, having pursued the Indians all the way from Victoria and Linnville, arrived at Plum Creek with about 125 volunteers.

The men set up camp for the night. Great numbers of loose animals were being herded together on the prairie. Later in the afternoon a cool shower provided some relief from the intense August heat.[34] That night the men sat around the campfire and told of personal experiences during the fight. As the men discussed the events of the day, a most unusual incident took place which was related by Robert Hall:

> The Tonkawas brought in the dead body of a Comanche warrior, and they built a big fire not far from where I was lying. My wound had begun to pain me considerably, and I did not pay much attention to them for some time. After awhile they began to sing and dance, and I thought that I detected the odor of burning flesh. I raised up and looked around, and, sure enough, our allies were cooking the Comanche warrior. They cut him into slices and broiled him on sticks. Curiously enough the eating of the flesh acted upon them as liquor does upon other men. After a few mouthfuls they began to act as if they were very drunk, and I don't think there was much pretense or sham about it. They danced, raved, howled, and sang, and invited me to get up and eat a slice of Comanche. They said it would make me brave. I was very hungry, but not sufficiently so to become a cannibal. The Tonkawas were wild over the victory and they did not cease their celebration until sunrise.[35]

The Comanches lost over eighty of their chiefs and warriors in the fight with the Texans at Plum Creek. Colonel Burleson initially reported that more than sixty Indians were killed. But during the day, as more parties of volunteers returned with additional reports, it became evident that more than eighty Indians had been killed. Eight or ten bodies of dead Comanches were found in the San Marcos River; several bodies were located as far away as the San Antonio Road. It is probable that, after returning to their camp, many other Indians died from wounds inflicted during the fight. For many years afterwards, bones of the Comanches were found along their path of retreat.[36]

Texan losses were slight. Major General Huston reported that the volunteers "lost one killed and seven wounded — one mortally." The Texan killed was Mr. DeWolf. The seven men wounded were Robert Hall, Henry McCulloch, Archibald Gibson, Columbus DeWitt, Dr. Alonzo B. Sweitzer, James Nichols,[37] and Samuel Hutchinson Reed.[38]

During the Indians' retreat a number of squaws and Indian children were captured by the Texans. One small child was found in a thicket about fifteen miles from Plum Creek. The volunteers heard the child crying, and although many of the men thought the noise was a ruse to lead them into ambush, one man entered the wooded area and rescued the child. The young boy, it was soon learned, was a child of the head chief of the Comanches. He was adopted by Judge Edmund Bellinger but lived for only a few months.[39]

The destruction of the formidable Comanche-Kiowa aggregation at Plum Creek was a severe blow to the Indians, one from which they would never fully recover. After this fight, the Indians never posed a major threat to the Central Texas area, nor did they ever penetrate into or below the settled portions of Texas again. However, the Indians did continue minor forays along the frontier for years afterwards. During night raids, small parties of Indians would steal horses and other livestock. On certain occasions women and children were killed. Anyone traveling alone or in small groups risked the danger of an Indian attack. But after the Battle of Plum Creek, the Indians, unless forced to fight, were reluctant to attack larger bodies of citizens or soldiers.

☆ 6

Moore's Victory on the Upper Colorado

In spite of their crushing defeat, the Indians continued minor depredations, making the frontier region unsafe for settlement. Many Texans believed that the Indians had not been punished severely enough for their devastating foray into the lower settlements. The Texans agreed that further chastisement was necessary to show that they would no longer tolerate the hostility of belligerent tribes residing within the boundaries of Texas. The government, in agreement with the settlers, was determined to show the Indians "that it had the power and would chastise them whenever the occasion required." [1]

Following the Battle of Plum Creek, Col. John H. Moore began circulating advertisements throughout the settlements in an effort to raise a volunteer force to pursue the Indians who had escaped at Plum Creek. Moore's plan was to penetrate the Comanche territory on the upper Colorado River and to seek out and destroy the enemy. Advertisements calling for volunteers were placed in many of the newspapers, the following being typical:

ATTENTION VOLUNTEERS!

The patriotic Citizens Soldiers intending to accompany the expedition against the hostile Indians on our Western frontier, are hereby notified, that the time of rendezvousing at

49

La Grange has been changed from the 10th to the 20th of
September.
  By order of the President
            JOHN H. MOORE, Col.–Comm't.
    LaGrange, Aug. 28, 1840. — 43:31[2]

Moore's circular advertisements brought a prompt response. By early October, between eighty and ninety men,
mostly from Fayette and Bastrop counties, had answered the
call for volunteers and had arrived in Austin. While there,
Moore received his orders from Secretary of War Branch T.
Archer. On Monday, October 5, the expedition, accompanied
by Chief Castro and seventeen Lipan Indians, left Walnut
Creek and proceeded up the Colorado River. After reaching
the headwaters of the San Gabriel River, the expedition
moved northwest toward the San Saba River. Along the way,
Moore had the Lipan scouts search the country, both right
and left, for Indian signs. As the Texans proceeded toward the
Concho River, they encountered disagreeable weather. A
Texas norther, accompanied with cold rain and icy winds,
brought adverse conditions to the men and the land. A number of the volunteers became sick, and one man, Garrett Harrell, died.[3]
  From the Concho, Moore's expedition directed its course
to the Colorado. Colonel Moore reported that the land along
the Colorado was very beautiful and fertile and offered a per-
fect place for settlement. Here the Lipan scouts found a large
Indian trail leading up the Red Fork of the Colorado. The
Texans began following the trail, and on October 23 they
found where the Indians "had been cutting pecan trees for the
fruit." [4]
  From the visible signs, Moore concluded that the Indians' encampment was not far away. The cold north wind had
been blowing all morning, and the men were permitted to seek
shelter underneath a hill. Colonel Moore then chose two of his
most expert Lipan scouts to examine the countryside. The
scouts left at about 10:30 A.M. and remained gone all day. As
evening approached, the Lipan chief grew uneasy over the
safety of his scouts. Climbing a high hill nearby to stand as a
lookout for his men, he soon informed the Texans that the

scouts were approaching at a distance of two or three miles. Having seen their shield signal, he reported that the scouts had located the Indians' camp.[5]

Receiving the news of the discovery of the Comanche village, the Texans, forgetting the bitter cold, were eager for a general engagement. After eating supper, the men proceeded north for about ten miles to the Colorado River. From there the Texans moved about four miles up the river. At this point the men secured their commissary of beef cattle on a mesquite flat near the river. The Texans continued their march for about four more miles, and at midnight the expedition reached a hollow near the river. The men were ordered to dismount, and Colonel Moore dispatched two scouts to the Comanche village to determine the location and strength of the enemy. At about 3:00 A.M. the scouts returned and reported that the Indians' encampment was located on the south bank of the river. From the number of tents the spies estimated that there were approximately sixty families and one hundred and twenty-five warriors. The Texans continued their advance on the Indian village. Within two miles of the Indian encampment, the volunteers secured their pack animals in a hollow. At daylight, on October 24, Moore ordered his men to mount and move forward. As the men approached the Comanche village, Colonel Moore ordered Lt. Clarke L. Owen to choose fifteen men "to act as cavalry, to cut off any retreat of the enemy." Capt. Thomas J. Rabb and his command were placed on the right; Clarke Owen occupied the center; and the volunteers under Capt. Nicholas M. Dawson were on the left.[6]

The volunteers moved within 200 yards of the enemy's encampment without being detected. Moore ordered Lieutenant Owen's cavalry to move to the right of Captain Rabb's company, and then the whole command, under Moore, charged the Indian camp. The Comanches were taken by complete surprise and fled to the river, "which was in the shape of a half moon encircling the village." As the troops charged into the village, they fired on the retreating and confused Indians. Halfway through the enemy's camp, the Texans dismounted but continued their deadly fire. Many of the Indians were killed before they were able to reach the river; a large number of others were killed or drowned as they ran into the water. A portion of the Comanches successfully reached the opposite side of the river and attempted to retreat across the prairie. Lieutenant Owen, who had been ordered to cross the river and cut off the enemy's retreat, executed his orders perfectly.[7]

Along the riverbank the Texans' fire was continued for about thirty minutes. As the Indians reached the opposite bank, the volunteers proved their marksmanship: "The river and its banks now presented every evidence of a total defeat. . . . The bodies of men, women and children were to be seen on every hand wounded, dying and dead." Having concluded the fight in the Comanche village, the volunteers pursued the remaining Indians for approximately four miles across the prairie. Soon the men returned and reported "that the enemy was entirely defeated." [8]

Although an honest effort was made to spare the lives of the women and children, a number of them were killed amidst the confusion of the fight. Many of the women fought along with the warriors and were killed. At one point in the Texan charge, Capt. Isaac N. Mitchell's bridle bit separated. Then the mule on which he was riding ran into the midst of the Indians and began to balk. A squaw ran up to Mitchell and, with a wooden club, knocked him from the mule. As Mitchell turned around, the squaw came at him with a large knife. The captain's companions shouted, "Kill her, Mitchell!" But the captain replied: "Oh, no, boys, I can't kill a woman!" Although the squaw was not killed, Mitchell was compelled to knock her to the ground in an effort to force the knife from her hand.[9]

During the fight, Judge Eastland and Charles Shuff encountered a Comanche boy who was about fourteen years old. The boy, who refused to surrender, defended himself boldly. At first the men intended to kill the Indian, but when they realized that he was only a young boy, they decided to capture him if possible. Even after the men had surrounded him, the boy grabbed a mesquite limb and forced the Texans to remain at a "respectable distance" by "flailing right and left as they endeavored to catch him." In order to save the men the trouble of capturing the boy alive, one of the Texans decided to shoot the Indian. As the man raised his rifle "Judge Eastland interposed and knocked it up, claiming that the boy deserved to be spared for his bravery and pluck." [10]

Moore's victory on the Colorado was the most severe punishment the Comanches had ever received from the Texans. The Indians were totally defeated in the fight. After examining the battle area, Colonel Moore reported that forty-eight Indians had been "killed upon the ground, and eighty killed and drowned in the river." This estimate, according to many of the Texans, was too small. [11]

In the fight with the Comanches no Texans were killed. Colonel Moore reported that two men, Mr. Daugherty of Colorado County and M. F. Jones of Fayette County, were slightly wounded. He also stated that two of the Texans' horses were wounded.

As the Texans regrouped at the Comanche village, it was discovered that thirty-four prisoners had been taken during the fight. Seven of these prisoners escaped during a stampede as the expedition made its way back to Austin. Three other prisoners were left behind by Colonel Moore. Also recaptured were two Mexican boys who had been taken by the Indians in a raid along the Rio Grande. The boys were fourteen and sixteen years old and had been captives for about three months. [12]

All of the Indians' property was either captured or destroyed by the Texans. Approximately 300 saddles and a great number of various kinds of skins and pelts were found in the Indian camp. Since much of this plunder was too cumbersome to carry back to Austin, it was burned by the troops. The volunteers also herded together a *caballado* of 500 horses captured from the enemy. These were taken with the Texans when they returned. [13]

On their return trip the volunteers carried back much camp equipage. Among these spoils taken by the Texans were goods recognized as those stolen by the Indians in the raid on Linnville. There was little doubt that the Indians defeated by Moore's volunteers had been involved in the raids on Victoria and Linnville.

By 10:00 A.M. the men had all returned and gathered in

the Indian village. Moore ordered the entire encampment, as well as all the Indians' property, to be burned. Within fifteen minutes the village was destroyed, with the exception of one large wigwam, where the wounded Indians and several squaws were left.[15]

With the entire Comanche village in flames, Moore ordered his men to mount and prepare to begin their march back to Austin. The volunteers returned to where their beef cattle had been secured. After collecting the cattle, the men continued on for six miles and camped for the night. Because of adverse weather conditions, Moore's expedition was forced to remain in camp for two days. As weather conditions improved, the volunteer militia resumed its march. Near the old San Saba Mission, Moore's volunteers encountered a small party of fifteen Seratic Indians. The Indians told Castro, the Lipan chief, that they were "desirous to treat" with the white men. A consultation was held. The Indians reported that they were friendly toward the white man and that they wished to aid in the wars against the Comanches, whom they hated. They informed Colonel Moore that they represented their tribe of about 800 warriors, located "in the vicinity of the Rio Grande, between Santa Fé and Chihuahua." [16]

All along their route back to Austin the Texans were harassed by small parties of hostile Indians. In one instance, as the volunteers camped along the Pedernales River, the Indians crept past the sentries and stole several horses, "including the fine saddle mule of Colonel Moore." When the Indians gained some distance from the Texans' encampment, they gave a loud yell. The men were awakened by the shouts but, unable to find the Indians, once again retired. When the Texans awoke the following morning they found that the Indians had stolen four horses.[17]

On November 7 Colonel Moore's expedition arrived back in Austin with the news of a triumphant victory over the Comanches. The Texans returned with twenty-four Comanche prisoners, several hundred horses, and other plunder carried home by the volunteers. In honor of the great victory the citizens of the capital city held a dinner and ball for the members of the expedition. Almost all of the men attended the celebration. That night the Texans' horses were secured on a "ditched field below Waller's Creek." Confident that the Indians would not venture too close to Austin, guards were placed only at the gate. As the celebration was being held, a party of Indians crept around the field, "filled up the ditch, and stole thirty or forty horses!" Consequently, many of the men were forced to walk home.[18]

A number of the Indian women and children captured by Moore's volunteers were taken to Austin and placed in individuals' homes, where they were required to help with domestic duties. The young Indian boy, "who had wielded the mesquite brush so vigorously," was taken into the home of Monsieur Alphonse de Saligny, the French minister to the Republic of Texas. Eventually, the Indian boy gained the French consul's confidence and was given many privileges. Every afternoon the boy would tend and exercise Saligny's favorite horse by riding the horse over his usual rounds and returning each time. One day the boy took the horse out for exercise and began riding in a large circle, enlarging the circle until he disappeared from sight. Neither the boy nor the horse was ever seen again.[19]

Another Indian boy captured during the fight on the Colorado was taken home by Judge Eastland, who named him "Sam Houston." When the Texans returned, they were tired and dirty. Judge Eastland and Captain Dawson decided to go to the creek for a bath, and they took the young boy with them. Since the weather was cold, the men built a fire to heat some water. The Indian boy, unable to understand the white men, became disturbed at their actions. When the boy learned to speak English, he told the men that he had feared that they were going to boil him in the water. For several years the Indian boy remained with Judge Eastland and became very attached to his family. He was later returned to his tribe in an exchange of prisoners. The boy said that he would not live with his tribe, but that he would return. Many years later Sam was recognized by Col. John R. Baylor, a government agent among the Comanches. Baylor reported that the Indian had married an Indian girl and lived with the Comanche tribe. Shortly afterwards, "Sam Houston" and his whole family were killed while on a "thieving expedition." [20]

Moore's expedition to the regions of the upper Colorado brought triumphant results. The Comanches, who had previously raided into the lower settlements, were totally destroyed — either at the Battle of Plum Creek or in the fight on the Colorado. After these defeats, the Comanches were never able to fully recover, and thus, they moved northward out of the Central Texas area. These engagements may have represented the most severe punishment ever inflicted upon the Comanches in Texas. With these two battles the Texans felt that the raids on Victoria and Linnville finally had been avenged.

☆ 7

Results of the Comanche Defeat

The failure of the Comanche Raid of 1840 produced several significant results. The defeat of the Comanches thwarted the Mexican effort to employ the Indians of Texas as allies. Evolving from this series of events was the development of cavalry tactics, the use of repeating firearms, a display of vigorous spirit in Indian fighting, and the learning experience of future leaders in warfare.

General Canalizo, the Mexican commander at Matamoros, entertained the idea of retaking Texas by the use of Indian allies. Realizing his opportunity to capitalize on their desire for revenge, Canalizo devised a plan in which the Comanches would play a major role as well as avenge the deaths of their fallen chiefs in San Antonio. Canalizo's scheme called for the Comanches to make a great raid down the Colorado River to the Gulf of Mexico. In accordance with this plan the Cherokees were to raid into East Texas while the Wacos and Apaches moved down the Brazos into Central Texas. With this action Canalizo hoped to drive the settlers from Texas and retake the territory for Mexico. In support of these raids 3,000 Mexican cavalry, led by Canalizo and Woll, were to penetrate into Texas and capture Austin and San Antonio. The plunder and thousands of horses and mules taken

by the Comanches in their raids on Victoria and Linnville
were to be used in the more formidable raid specified in Canalizo's plan.[1]

Circumstances and some evidence indicate that Mexican
emissaries were sent among the Comanches not only to incite
them to make raids on the frontier settlements but also to aid
the Indians in their preparations for the raids.

The hostile Comanches were unaccustomed to making
forays into the lower settlements. Therefore, they were not fa-
miliar with the country. Unless they had been guided into this
unfamiliar territory by Mexicans, it is questionable whether
or not the Indians would have been able to avoid all Anglo
settlements and thus benefit from a surprise attack as at Victoria and Linnville. The fear-stricken citizens did not believe
"that a body of Indians would venture so low down the country, or could approach so near without some intelligence of the
fact." [2] Had the Indians not known exactly when and where
to strike, it is doubtful that they would have obtained such an
immense amount of plunder. The Indians' raids happened to
coincide with the arrival of a large number of horses. At the
time of the raid there were several Mexican traders in Victoria
with a herd of 500 horses for sale or trade. By nightfall the Indians had herded in over 1,500 horses and mules, many of
which belonged to a Mr. Sutherland, who was en route east to
sell his horses.[3]

With their immense *caballado* of horses and mules the Indians proceeded to Linnville. The Comanches spent the day
looting the many warehouses, which contained shipments of
supplies that had been brought from New Orleans for the
merchants of San Antonio. These supplies were either destroyed or were carried away by the Indians.[4] Approximately
$300,000 worth of goods were in Linnville at the time of the
raid. According to Ben McCulloch, the Indians carried with
them 3,000 horses and 700 pack mules loaded with plunder.[5]

It was no mere accident that the Indians happened to
choose Victoria and Linnville as targets for their raids. Nor
was it coincidence that the prairies were covered with horses
and the warehouses filled with supplies at the time.

Had this great raid been *merely* an effort on the part of the

Comanches to seek revenge on the Texans and to avenge the deaths of their chiefs at the Council House Fight, it is seriously doubtful that they would have strayed so far into the inhabited portions of Texas. A punitive raid on any of the exposed settlements or towns situated on the frontier would have been satisfactory. They could have quickly swept down upon Austin, Gonzales, or other vulnerable settlements along the frontier and then swiftly retired back to the safety of Comanchería.

This raid, in all probability, was conceived in Matamoros by the Centralists who had been, for some years, agitating the Indians and attempting to utilize them as allies to the Mexican cause. Their reasons for selecting Victoria and Linnville as targets for the Comanches' revenge were twofold — the most apparent being the large herds of horses and mules in the area and the richly laden warehouses in Linnville. Raids on these settlements would have been very profitable to the Indians and could have benefited the Centralists in future raids made by the Comanches.

Secondly, there were ulterior motives for the Centralists to direct the Indian attacks upon Victoria and Linnville. These reasons stemmed from domestic problems between themselves and the Federalists in Mexico. For years efforts had been made by Federalist leaders to break away from the centralistic form of government and revert back to the federal Constitution of 1824. This Federalist movement was particularly strong throughout the northern states of Mexico. With the failure of the Federalists in their efforts to reinstate the Constitution of 1824, a revolution erupted in northern Mexico. The Federalist leaders of Tamaulipas, Nuevo Leon, and Coahuila broke away from the Centralist government and organized a new confederation known as the Republic of the Rio Grande.[6] Jesús Cárdenas was chosen president and Antonio Canales was placed as commander-in-chief of the army.[7] On March 24–25, 1840, the Federalist army met with a disastrous defeat at the hands of the Centralist general, Mariano Arista, in the battle of Santa Rita de Morelos.[8] This defeat prompted General Canales to retreat into Texas, and in April he arrived on the Medina River with remnants of his forces.[9] On April 7 President Cárdenas established his provisional

government headquarters at Victoria. The Federalists had retreated into Texas seeking refuge and hoping to negotiate with
the government of the Republic for aid to continue their fight
against the Centralists.[10]

Although the Republic of Texas was never to grant official recognition to the newly organized Republic of the Rio
Grande, many of its citizens embraced the Federalist cause. In
Victoria and along much of the South Texas frontier, Cárdenas and his followers were well received and encountered a
sympathetic audience for their struggle against the Centralist
government.

On April 11 the citizens of Victoria held a large public
dinner in honor of the officials of the Cárdenas government.
Huge numbers of people turned out to show their support and
express their sympathies for the Federalist struggle. The
crowd was so large that not all could be seated. The elabo-
rately prepared dinner was followed with the finest cham-
pagne and the presentation of numerous toasts. Even the old
twelve-pounder owned by the people of Victoria was fired in
honor of this special occasion.[11]

Throughout the month of April, the provisional government of the Republic of the Rio Grande recruited volunteers
and amassed a considerable amount of supplies to continue
their revolution. Many of these supplies obviously were received through Linnville, which served as the port of entry for
most goods destined for Victoria. Besides the stores of domestic goods and merchandise being shipped to Linnville, there
were also large quantities of munitions, powder, and cannon
to be found there.[12]

The immense stocks of merchandise being accumulated
at Victoria "in anticipation of a lucrative traffic with the Mexicans," [13] the packed warehouses of domestic and military
goods at Linnville, and the enthusiastic acceptance and ar-
dent support extended to the Federalists were all contributing
factors in the Centralists directing the Comanches' revenge
against Victoria and Linnville.

After the Battle of Plum Creek, much of the booty recaptured from the Indians was divided among the participants in
the fight. One man, James N. Smith, received a beautiful

beaded shot bag with Roman cross designs on it. An examination of the contents of the bag revealed a letter written from a Mexican to one of the Indian chiefs. In the letter the Mexican stated that "they would meet each other at Corpus Christi or Lynvill *(sic)*."[14]

During their raid, the Comanches very cautiously avoided a fight. They seemed to be more interested in the plunder taken on their foray. The Indians' principal interest in their horses and pack animals tends to indicate that there was a need for the goods, possibly to be used in a larger and more formidable raid on the frontier settlements. It is apparent that throughout the entire raid the Comanches were more interested in collecting plunder than in murder and revenge. Immediately after attacking Victoria, the Indians gathered up the large numbers of horses on the prairies. At Linnville the Comanches were more interested in the goods found in the stores and warehouses than they were in murdering the townspeople.[15]

Burdened with immense plunder, the Comanches began a slow retreat northward. Although a group of Texans under Capt. John Tumlinson attempted to engage the Indians in battle, the Comanches showed a disposition to avoid fighting. They were more interested in getting their horses and plunder to the safety of the Hill Country. The Indians would encircle the Texans and skirmish with them while their plunder was pushed onward.[16]

When the Comanches were confronted by the Texas volunteers at Plum Creek, they once again tried to avoid a battle. The Indians immediately formed a line between their plunder and the Texans. As a number of Comanche warriors engaged the Texans in minor skirmishing, the major portion of the war party, along with captives, plunder, and horses, continued across the prairie. It was only after the Texans charged that the Indians were forced to fight.[17] Many of the volunteers could not understand why the Indians refused to fight. One Texan stated:

> It has always been a mystery to me why the Indians became so terribly demoralized in this battle. It was fought on the open prairie, and they could easily see that they greatly out-

numbered us. It is rather strange that they did not make a stand.[18]

Following the Battle of Plum Creek, Major General Huston reported that a Mr. Sutherland

> had information from a Mexican, that the expedition was gotten up at Matamoros, and was to be composed of six hundred Indians and forty Mexicans; and this is confirmed by the fact that new Mexican blankets and other articles usually given as presents to the Indians, were found amongst the plunder.[19]

After the Great Comanche Raid, the only major depredation made by the Comanches was carried out against the Mexicans in the states of Coahuila and Nuevo Leon, the latter suffering most severely. It is believed that this raid into Mexico resulted from the failure of the Mexicans to send promised support to the Comanches in their raids on Victoria and Linnville.[20] An account of this raid is given by Captain Flack:

> In October, 1840, more than four hundred warriors penetrated into Mexico some four hundred miles, and killed, scalped, burned and destroyed everything they could; their track could be traced for miles by the burning ranches and villages.[21]

As a result of this raid, the state of Nuevo Leon lost approximately 700 inhabitants, and Coahuila lost almost the same number. Many women were captured, and thousands of horses and other livestock were stolen.[22]

Col. Reuben M. Potter, who resided in Matamoros at the time of the Great Comanche Raid, stated that "there are many circumstances connected with the raids on Victoria and Linnville which support the claim that Mexican authorities instigated them and promised co-operation in carrying them out." [23]

Felix Huston's victory at Plum Creek and Colonel Moore's victory on the upper Colorado utterly crushed the fighting power of the Comanches in Central Texas. These overwhelming victories also frustrated Canalizo's plans for retaking Texas with the help of Indian allies. The Comanches' defeat helped to ease the constant threat of the most powerful and most feared Indian tribe in Central Texas. Believing that the Texans were invincible, the Comanches never attempted to molest the Central Texas settlers to any great extent after 1840. Since the most powerful Indian tribe involved in the Mexican plot had been defeated, the whole scheme was abandoned.

It is significant that, with the defeat of the Comanches, there came the development of new tactics in frontier warfare against the Indians. Until the Great Comanche Raid, it was highly irregular for the Texans to charge a large body of Indians. The usual procedure for the volunteer soldiers was to dismount and await the Indians' charge or attack. These tactics were employed by John Tumlinson's men as they followed the Comanches toward Plum Creek, but were changed by Huston as the battle progressed.[24]

The Battle of Plum Creek began with the Texans employing the usual ploys of Indian fighting. Major General Huston's plan of action called for his men to dismount and form a hollow square with one side open. When it was realized that this form of fighting was ineffective, Huston ordered a general charge. Firing as they charged, the men advanced on the Indians. "The Indians did not stand the charge, and fled at all points."[25]

In Moore's fight on the upper Colorado, cavalry tactics were also used effectively. Moore's volunteers charged directly into the Indian village, firing their guns from horseback. As the enemy fled, Lt. Clarke Owen's men, acting as a cavalry unit, pursued the Indians and cut off their retreat. These men also fired from horseback. In this fight Captain Andrews tested one of Colt's repeating rifles and reported that he was able to fire the Colt rifle ten times while his companions were able to fire their rifles only twice.[26]

The Battle of Plum Creek and the fight on the upper Colorado marked the beginning of a new era in frontier warfare. Mounted charges, firing from horseback, and the use of repeating firearms all helped to establish cavalry as a potent weapon against the Plains Indians.[27]

With the defeat of the Comanches, a new spirit was exhibited by the Texans. There was more determination and enthusiasm in the men's actions. Huston reported at Plum Creek that "nothing could exceed the animation of the men." It was also reported that Burleson exhibited "cool, deliberate and prompt courage and conduct." The other leaders had also "acted with the utmost courage and firmness." [28]

John Moore, who led the expedition against the Comanches on the upper Colorado, reported that his commanders displayed "gallant and officer-like conduct and bearing during the entire campaign, and particularly during the engagement." [29]

Until the Great Comanche Raid, this new and exhilarating spirit displayed by the Texans was not present. Before 1840, the Texans showed little enthusiasm in Indian fighting. In previous Indian fights the Texans were usually hampered by negligence, incompetence, and failure. At Plum Creek, however, no mistakes were made, although Huston would have failed to deliver such a crushing blow to the Comanches had it not been for the advice of older and more experienced Indian fighters like Caldwell, Burleson, and McCulloch. Colonel Moore's expedition into Comanche territory was a successful achievement. His appropriate orders and the troops' swift and accurate performance resulted in a total defeat for the Comanches. These battles helped to develop experienced Indian fighters and produce competent leaders who would later take an active part in the Mexican War and the Civil War.[30]

The Great Comanche Raid of 1840 ended in disaster for the Indians. The Comanches were completely surprised and overwhelmed by Texan forces at Plum Creek and on the upper Colorado River. These two fights resulted in sweeping victories for the Texans. The Comanches, considered to be the fiercest of all Indians in Texas, were utterly crushed and never recovered from their defeat. The Great Comanche Raid of 1840 was the last major threat to the settlers in the South Central Texas area, although minor skirmishes and depredations continued in the region for some years afterwards. The Comanche defeat introduced "an important epoch in Texas history, and indeed most of our historians regard it as the turning point in affairs with the Indians." [31]

Since Indian problems had hindered the settlement of the Texas frontier for many years, the defeat of the Indians in the Great Comanche Raid helped to accelerate the westward movement. Had it not been for the Great Comanche Raid, the Battle of Plum Creek, and Moore's victory on the Colorado River, the westward settlement of the Texas frontier would probably have been drastically retarded in the nineteenth century. The defeat of the hostile Comanches aided greatly in making the uninhabitable frontier of Texas a safe place for the settlers to build homes and raise families.

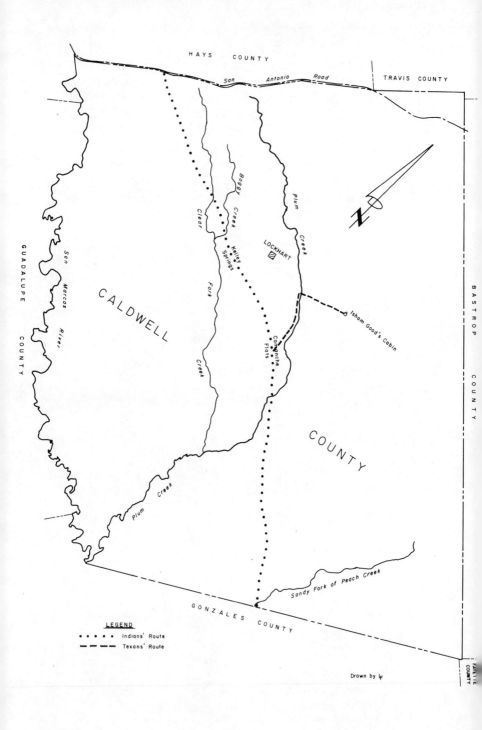

HAYS COUNTY
TRAVIS COUNTY
San Antonio Road
BASTROP COUNTY
GUADALUPE COUNTY
San Marcos River
CALDWELL
Clear
Boggy Creek
Fork
Kelley Springs
LOCKHART
Plum Creek
COUNTY
Comanche Flats
Isham Good's Cabin
Creek
Plum Creek
Sandy Fork of Peach Creek
GONZALES COUNTY
FAYETTE COUNTY

N

LEGEND
• • • • • Indians' Route
– – – – Texans' Route

Drawn by LF

Appendix A

Participants in Cordova Fight, March 28, 1839

Annotated list of names of men who served with Col. Edward Burleson's command in the Cordova Fight of March 28, 1839, on Mill Creek near Seguin. The original list was taken from the *Telegraph and Texas Register*, April 17, 1839.

Adkisson, A. J.
Alderson, Henry
Alexander, Pleasant Duke
Allen, George
Andrews, Micah
Barnhart, Joseph
Barton, Wayne
Bennett, Spius C.
Billingsley, Jesse
Brown, A. E.
Brown, John W.
Burleson, Edward
Burleson, John
Burleson, Jonathan
Byers, Ross
Caldwell, John
Campbell, B. A.
Carter, William
Childress, Hugh M.
Clopton, William A.
Colver, Samuel
Conley, Preston
Conn, Napoleon
Crocheron, Henry
Cunningham, J. R.
Dancer, John
Durst, John G.
Eakin, John J.
Engelhart, Lewis
Fentress, James

Flesher, Nelson
Foster, John L.
Gillet, S. S.
Gilmore, D. C.
Glascock, G. J.
Gorman, James P.
Hardeman, Owen Bailey
Hardeman, William Polk
Haynie, Dr. S. G.
Hemphill, Cornelius M.
Hemphill, William A.
Hicks, M.
Highsmith, Samuel
Holmes, William
Hornsby, Malcolm M.
Hornsby, William M.
Johnson, Enoch S.
Lester, James S.
Lloyd, Richard J.
Lynch, John L.
McGary, Isaac
McKernon, Thomas
Mabry, James L.
Miller, James
Miller, R. M.
Mills, Richard M.
Moore, John
Moore, Thomas
Morgan, H. S.
Newcomb, William

Norris, Isaac
Pendleton, John W.
Rice, James O.
Robinson, John B.
Robison, J. N.
Robison, W. M.
Sanders, Thomas
Scott, George W.
Sharp, G. W.

Shelp, Daniel C.
Smith, J. L.
Turner, Winslow
Vandever, Logan
Walker, Martin
Whiting, F. P.
Wilson, ———
Woods, Henry Gonzalvo

Appendix B

Texan Casualties in Comanche Raid, August 1840

List of known Texan casualties incurred during the Comanche raid on the lower settlements of Victoria and Linnville in August 1840.

Killed

Bell, Dr. John F.
Caldwell, Pinckney Coatsworth
Crosby, ——— (infant)
Daniels, ———
Foley, Tucker
Gray, Dr. Arthur
Mordecai [Mordica], Benjamin H.
Nuner, William McMin
O'Neill, Joseph
Richeson, Varlan

Smart, George
Stephens, ———
Watts, Hugh Oram
One Englishman (name unknown)
Eight Negroes (names unknown)
One Mexican (name unknown)

Wounded

Clausel, ———
Kraatz, Lewis
Menefee, John S.
Ponton, Dr. Joel

Appendix C

Participants in Battle of Plum Creek, August 12, 1840

Ackland, Christopher "Kit"
Anderson, Col. ———
Baker, John
Baylor, Robert Emmett Bledsoe

Beatty, Edward
Beitel, Joseph
Bell, Col. ———
Bellinger, Judge Edmund

Berry, Andrew Jackson
Berry, James
Berry, John Bates
Berry, Joseph
Billingsley, Jesse
Bird, James
Bird, Jonathan
Birdwell, William
Bostick, Sion Record
Braches, Charles
Brown, Dr. Caleb S.
Brown, Dr. David F.
Brown, John Henry
Burleson, Edward
Burleson, Jonathan
Burleson, Joseph, Jr.
Burnam, Jesse
Burnam, William Owen
Caldwell, Mathew
Carter, William J. S.
Chalk, Whitfield
Clopton, William
Cocke, James Decatur
Cordell, Owen N.
Cox, Rev. Thomas J.
Cushney, William H.
Darlington, John Washington
Darst, David S. H.
Day, Milford
Dees, Gordon
DeWees, William B.
DeWitt, C. C.
DeWolf, ———
Earnest, Felix B.
Fentress, Dr. James
Friar, Daniel Boone
Galbreath, Thomas
Gipson, Archibald
Gipson, James
Good, Isham Jones
Grover, George W.
Hall, Robert
Hankins, Eli Skaggs
Hardeman, Owen Bailey
Hardeman, Thomas Monroe
Hardeman, William P.

Haynes, Charles
Hays, John Coffee "Jack"
Highsmith, Benjamin Franklin
Hill, A. W.
Hornsby, Joe
Howard, George Thomas
Humphreys, Jacob Jackson
Husbands, ———
Huston, Felix
Izod, James
Jenkins, John Holland
Jones, Col. Henry
Lawrence, Joseph
Lee, Nelson
Litton, Addison
Litton, Frank M.
McCoy, John
McCulloch, Benjamin
McCulloch, Henry Eustace
McCulloch, Samuel
Magill, James P.
Magill, William Harrison
Miller, Alsey S.
Mills, James L.
Moon, William Washington
Morrell, Rev. Z. N.
Moss, James
Murphree, David
Neill, Andrew
Neill, George
Nichols, James Wilson
Nichols, John
Nichols, Thomas
Ogsbury, Charles A.
Oury, William Sanders
Patton, James
Perry, Rufus Cicero
Pilgrim, Thomas J.
Placido
Porter, Elijah R.
Randall, Barney
Randle, Wilson
Redfield, Henry Prentice
Reid, Samuel Hutchinson
Rice, James O.
Roberts, Alexander "Buck"

Rodarmel, Lemuel M.
Rogers, Henry
Rogers, John A., Jr.
Rogers, John A., Sr.
Rogers, Samuel C. A.
Scarborough, William L.
Short, Thomas W.
Smith, Ezekiel
Smith, French
Smith, James N.
Smith, John L.
Sowell, Andrew
Sowell, John
Stapp, Darwin M.
Stapp, Oliver H.
Stem, Isaac Phillip
Sweitzer, Dr. Alonzo B.
Taylor, Creed

Thompson, Barry
Thurmond, Alfred S.
Wagner, ———
Wallace, Joseph Washington Elliot
Wallace, William A. A. "Bigfoot"
Waller, Judge Edwin
Ward, Lafayette
Wheeler, Jesse O.
White, David N.
White, John M.
White, Newton
White, Peter
White, Sam Addison
White, Simon C.
Wilburn, Caleb
Winchel, Henry C.
Wright, Charles Jno.

Appendix D

Participants in Col. John H. Moore's Expedition to Upper Colorado River, October 1840

Alexander, Darwin S.
Andrews, Micah
Baylor, Henry Weidner
Baylor, John Robert
Blackburn, Andrew J.
Breeding, Benjamin W.
Breeding, John
Browne, Lionel
Burnham, Jesse
Burnham, John H.
Calhoun, Julian C.
Caruthers, Williams
Castro
Crownover, Arter
Dale, Elijah V.
Dancy, John W.

Darling, Socrates
Daugherty, Burton M.
Dawson, Nicholas Mosby
Day, John H.
Dickerson, Lewis W.
Dodd, John
Earthman, Henry
Eastland, Nicholas W.
Elliott, Jacob
Elly, Gustav
Evans, William M.
Faison, Nathaniel W.
Fields, Smallwood S. B.
Foley, Mason B.
Gardenier, A. A.
Gillespie, M. M.

Gillespie, Richard Addison
Habermill, George
Harrell, Garrett
Harrell, Leander
Hayden, Gerrard
Heard, William Jones Elliot
Hill, James M.
Holcomb, Erwin
Holman, John T.
Hudson, David
Hudson, James P.
Hunt, William G.
James, Thomas D.
Jones, Griffith H.
Jones, Myers F.
Keene, Richard H.
Kornegay, David S.
Lawrence, Joseph
Long, William
Longley, James P.
Lubbock, Thomas S.
Lynch, Addison
Lyons, DeWitt C.
McAnnelly, Pleasant
McGuffin, John F.
Menefee, Thomas S.
Mercer, Elijah G.

Mitchell, Isaac N.
Mitchell, William
Moore, A. L. D.
Moore, John Henry
Nail, L. M.
Nail, William A.
Nelson, G. H.
Penick, Thomas M.
Rabb, Thomas J.
Rector, Pendleton
Redfield, Henry Prentice
Robinson, William M.
Rockyfeller, Peter
Ryan, Nicholas J.
Scallorn, Newton
Scheoff [Shuff], Charles
Shaw, Josiah
Shaw, Peter V.
Simons, Joseph
Smith, James A. J.
Snelling, John O.
Spencer, William
Thompson, Jasper McD. N.
Vogle, Frederick
Wells, John A.
Williams, Charles
Woods, Henry Gonzalvo
Wright, Charles

CHIEF BOWLES — *Cherokee leader killed July 16, 1839, at the Battle of the Neches.*

VALENTIN CANALIZO — *Mexican Centralist leader who succeeded Gen. Vicente Filisola as commandant of the northern forces and promoted a Mexican-Indian alliance to retard the settlement of the Texas frontier.*

MIRABEAU B. LAMAR — *President of the Republic of Texas (1838–1841) who initiated the aggressive anti-Indian policy which led to the expulsion of the Cherokees, the Council House Fight, the Comanche Raid of 1840, and the defeats of the Comanches at Plum Creek and on the upper Colorado River.*

JESSE BILLINGSLEY — *Captain of a portion of the Texan force engaged in the Cordova Fight near Seguin on March 28, 1839, and later a participant in the Battle of Plum Creek.*

COUNCIL HOUSE — *Site of the Council House Fight in San Antonio where twelve Comanche chiefs were slain on March 19, 1840, thus precipitating the Comanche raids on Victoria and Linnville.*

GEORGE T. HOWARD — *Captain of a company of Texas Militia at the Council House Fight. Although wounded in this fight, Captain Howard recovered in time to participate in the Battle of Plum Creek.*

DR. JOEL PONTON — *Seriously wounded by Indians as they made their way into the lower settlements, Ponton narrowly escaped death and sounded the alarm of impending danger.*

SITE OF LINNVILLE — *The early port town of Linnville was burned by the Comanches on August 8, 1840.*

MAJ. GEN. FELIX HUSTON — *Elected commander of the Texas forces against the Comanches at the Battle of Plum Creek.*

EDWARD BURLESON — *Leader of a group of Texans and Tonkawa Indians from the Bastrop area who participated in the Battle of Plum Creek.*

PLACIDO — *Chief of the Tonkawa Indians who allied with the Texans against the Comanches at the Battle of Plum Creek.*

THOMAS MONROE HARDEMAN — *Shared in the command of a portion of the Texan forces at the Battle of Plum Creek.*

COMANCHE FLATS — *Site of the initial contact between the Texan forces and the Comanches at Plum Creek in Caldwell County.*

KELLEY SPRINGS — *View of the area where the most concentrated fighting in the Battle of Plum Creek occurred.*

BENJAMIN McCULLOCH — *One of the seasoned Indian fighters who participated in the Battle of Plum Creek. He later distinguished himself in the Mexican War and eventually rose to the rank of brigadier general in the Confederate Army.*

HENRY McCULLOCH — *Indian fighter and Texas Ranger, Henry McCulloch served as a captain in the Mexican War and attained the rank of brigadier general during the Civil War, as did his brother.*

ALSEY S. MILLER — *A participant in the Battle of Plum Creek.*

ROBERT HALL — *One of the Texans who was wounded at the Battle of Plum Creek.*

DR. DAVID F. BROWN — *One of the men from Bastrop who fought at Plum Creek. With the assistance of the Reverend Z. N. Morrell, Dr. Brown extracted the arrow which wounded Mrs. Watts, who had been captured by the Indians at Linnville.*

Residence of JULIET C. WATTS FRETWELL, *Port Lavaca.*

INDIAN HEADDRESS — *Buffalo cap headdress taken off a slain Comanche warrior at the Battle of Plum Creek.*

TEXIAN RIFLE — *Percussion rifle used by Dr. James Fentress in the Cordova Fight in 1839 and in the Battle of Plum Creek.*

J. W. DARLINGTON — *Participant in the Battle of Plum Creek.*

WILLIAM P. HARDEMAN — *Prominent figure throughout the Republic of Texas who participated in countless engagements with the Indians, including the Plum Creek fight.*

JOHN C. HAYS — *Most noted for his exploits as a Texas Ranger, Hays participated in his first Indian battle at Plum Creek against the Comanches. He became one of the most famous Texas Ranger captains and served as a colonel during the Mexican War.*

WILLIAM W. MOON — *Participant in the Battle of Plum Creek.*

ALEXANDER "BUCK" ROBERTS — *Fought in the Battle of Plum Creek. His son, Dan W. Roberts, later became a famous Texas Ranger captain.*

JOHN HENRY MOORE — *Led the expedition against the Comanches on the upper Colorado River in November 1840. This successful raid helped to drive the Comanches farther north onto the High Plains of Texas.*

CLARKE L. OWEN — *Commander of a portion of the Texan force led against the Comanches on the upper Colorado River by John H. Moore.*

PUBLIC DEBT RECORD — *Compensation awarded Nicholas M. Dawson for services rendered as captain on the John H. Moore expedition against the Comanches in 1840. Dawson was killed on September 18, 1842, at the Battle of Salado, while leading a company of Texans against the invading Mexican forces under Adrian Woll.*

Photographic Credits

Battle of Plum Creek: Painting by Lee Herring. Owned by Bill Adams of Dallas, Texas. Painting located in the Institute of Texan Cultures, San Antonio, Texas.

Chief Bowles: From *The Indian Papers of Texas and the Southwest 1825–1916*, *Vol. I*, edited by Dorman Winfrey and James Day, 1966, frontispiece. Courtesy Jenkins Publishing Company, Austin, Texas.

Valentin Canalizo: From *The Eagle: The Autobiography of Santa Anna*, edited by Ann Fears Crawford (1967), 178. Courtesy Jenkins Publishing Company, Austin, Texas.

Mirabeau B. Lamar: Courtesy Archives Division, Texas State Library, 1987/97-1.

Jesse Billingsley: Prints and Photograph Collection, Courtesy Barker Texas History Center, University of Texas at Austin.

Council House: Sketch by artist Raymond Vásquez. Courtesy Richard G. Santos, San Antonio, Texas.

George T. Howard: Prints and Photograph Collection, Courtesy Barker Texas History Center, University of Texas at Austin.

Dr. Joel Ponton: Courtesy Mrs. Fannie Ponton, Corpus Christi, Texas.

Site of Linnville: Photograph in collection of the author.

Maj. Gen. Felix Huston: Courtesy Archives Division, Texas State Library, 1/102-310.

Edward Burleson: Courtesy Archives Division, Texas State Library, 1979/181-1.

Placido: From *Indian Depredations in Texas* by J. W. Wilbarger, 1888, opposite p. 368.

Thomas Monroe Hardeman: Prints and Photograph Collection, Courtesy Barker Texas History Center, University of Texas at Austin.

Battle of Plum Creek: From *Indian Depredations in Texas* by J. W. Wilbarger, 1888, opposite p. 25.

Comanche Flats: Photograph courtesy John Anderson, Austin, Texas.

Kelley Springs: Photograph courtesy John Anderson, Austin, Texas.

Benjamin McCulloch: Courtesy Archives Division, Texas State Library, 1963/283-33.

Henry McCulloch: Courtesy Archives Division, Texas State Library, 1/102-378.

Alsey S. Miller: Courtesy Mrs. Lucy Ainsworth, Luling, Texas.

Robert Hall: Lawrence T. Jones Collection, Courtesy Lawrence T. Jones III, Austin, Texas.

Dr. David F. Brown: Courtesy Mrs. Helen Rugeley, Austin, Texas.

Residence of Juliet C. Fretwell: Photograph in collection of the author.

Indian Headdress: Courtesy Cincinnati Museum of Natural History, Cincinnati, Ohio (Artifact A 13144).

Texian Rifle: Courtesy Daughters of the Republic of Texas, The Alamo, San Antonio, Texas.

J. W. Darlington: Prints and Photograph Collection, Courtesy Barker Texas History Center, University of Texas at Austin.

William P. Hardeman: Prints and Photograph Collection, Courtesy Barker Texas History Center, University of Texas at Austin.

John C. Hays: Prints and Photograph Collection, Courtesy Barker Texas History Center, University of Texas at Austin.

William W. Moon: Prints and Photograph Collection, Courtesy Barker Texas History Center, University of Texas at Austin.

Alexander "Buck" Roberts: Courtesy Ken Hyman, Leander, Texas.

John Henry Moore: Prints and Photograph Collection, Courtesy Barker Texas History Center, University of Texas at Austin.

Clarke L. Owen: Prints and Photograph Collection, Courtesy Barker Texas History Center, University of Texas at Austin.

Public Debt Record: Courtesy Archives Division, Texas State Library, Comptroller's Republic payments for service.

Map of Cherokee Land Grant: From *The Indian Papers of Texas and the Southwest 1825–1916, Vol. I*, edited by Dorman Winfrey and James Day

(1966) between pages 134–135. Courtesy Jenkins Publishing Company, Austin, Texas.

Comanche Country and Adjacent Territory, 1840: From *Comanche Barrier to South Plains Settlement* by R. N. Richardson, The Arthur H. Clark Company, Glendale (1933), 106–107. Reproduced by permission.

Route of the Great Comanche Raid of 1840: Map courtesy Linda Fields, Austin, Texas.

Route of the Battle of Plum Creek: Map courtesy Linda Fields, Austin, Texas.

Endnotes

(Note: Due to its frequent mention, the Texas State Library, Archives Division, Austin, Texas, is listed as TSL-A.)

INTRODUCTION

1. Hubert Howe Bancroft, *A History of the North Mexican States and Texas* (San Francisco: The History Company, Publishers, 1889), 2:315.
2. Asa Kyrus Christian, *Mirabeau Buonaparte Lamar* (Austin: Von Boeckmann-Jones Company, Printers, 1922), 3.
3. John D. Hicks, *The Federal Union: A History of the United States to 1865* (Cambridge, MA: Houghton Mifflin Company, Riverside Press, 1952), 354–355.
4. Christian, *Mirabeau Buonaparte Lamar*, 3.
5. Walter P. Webb, *The Texas Rangers: A Century of Frontier Defense* (Austin: University of Texas Press, 1935), 7.
6. *Ibid.*, 47–54.
7. Rupert N. Richardson, *The Comanche Barrier to South Plains Settlement* (Glendale, CA: The Arthur H. Clarke Company, 1938), 106–107.
8. Webb, *The Texas Rangers*, 55–57.
9. *Ibid.*, 45–46, 57–62.

Chapter 1:   MEXICAN INTERVENTION INTO INDIAN AFFAIRS

1. Webb, *The Texas Rangers*, 48.
2. Thomas Maitland Marshall, *A History of the Western Boundary of the Louisiana Purchase, 1819–1841* (Berkeley: University of California Press, 1914), 141–157, 172; "Testimony of Miguel de Cortínez, interpreted by Nathaniel Amory, communicated to Gen. Gaines, April 12, 1836," United States Congress, *Senate Executive Documents*, 25th Congress, 2d Session, XII, Doc. 351: 781–782; J[oseph] Bonnell to Maj. Gen. E. P. Gaines, April 20, 1836, *ibid.*, 774–775.
3. D. W. Smith to John Forsyth, Consulate of the U.S.A., Matamoros, January 6, 1837, No. 115, in Consular Dispatches (Texas), 1837–1839 (Matamoros), ms, microfilm; James Douglas to Hon. Wm. H. Wharton, December 23, 1838, United States Congress, *Senate Executive Documents*, 32d Congress, 2d Session, III, Doc. 14: 40–41.

4. According to Yoakum's *History of Texas,* Mexican agents circulated among the tribes of the frontier Indians of Texas during the spring of 1837 to incite the Indians. Henderson Yoakum, *History of Texas From Its First Settlement in 1685 to Its Annexation to the United States in 1846* (New York: J. S. Redfield, 1855), 2:227.

5. Webb, *The Texas Rangers,* 49.

6. Texas Congress, *Journal of the House of Representatives of the Republic of Texas,* 1st Congress, 2d Session, 12.

7. Vicente Cordova to Manuel Flores, July 19, 1838, Records Relating to Indian Affairs (RG 005), Series I: Indian Affairs as published in *The Indian Papers of Texas and the Southwest,* Doc. 2, TSL-A.

8. Anson Jones to John Forsyth, December 31, 1838, *Senate Executive Documents,* 32d [United States] Congress, 2d Session, III, Doc. 14: 11–12; "Memorandum Book," *ibid.,* 14–17.

9. *Telegraph and Texas Register* (Houston), October 27, 1838; R. A. Irion to Sam Houston, November 14, 1838, Letter Book #1, Department of State, November 12, 1836–January 10, 1842, 71, TSL-A.

10. "Memorandum Book," 14–17.

11. Jones to Forsyth, December 31, 1838, *Senate Executive Documents,* 32d [United States] Congress, 2d Session, III, Doc. 14: 11–12.

12. "Memorandum Book," 14–17.

13. Joseph Milton Nance, *After San Jacinto: The Texas-Mexican Frontier, 1836–1841* (Austin: University of Texas Press, 1963), 120–121.

14. Col. Hugh McLeod to Gen. M. B. Lamar, October 22, 1838, Mirabeau B. Lamar Papers, Doc. 846, TSL-A.

15. John Forsyth to Alcée La Branche, January 8, 1839; Alcée La Branche to John Forsyth, January 29, 1839; R. G. Dunlap to John Forsyth, May 29, 1839; Thomas J. Rusk to Sidney Johnston, February 25, 1839, in *Senate Executive Documents,* 32d [United States] Congress, 2d Session, III, Doc. 14: 18–25.

16. Valentin Canalizo to Manuel Flores and chiefs of the friendly nations, February 27, 1839, *Senate Executive Documents,* 32d [United States] Congress, 2d Session, III, Doc. 14: 31–32; Adjutant General Records (RG 401), Army Papers, TSL-A.

17. J. W. Wilbarger, *Indian Depredations in Texas* (Austin: Hutchins Printing House, 1889), 152; Canalizo to Flores and friendly nations, February 27, 1839, Adjutant General Records (RG 401), TSL-A.

18. According to one report there were fifty-three Mexicans, six Biloxi Indians, and five Negroes accompanying Cordova to Mexico. Edward Burleson to Mirabeau B. Lamar, April 4, 1838 [1839], Lamar Papers, Doc. 701, TSL-A. Another report states that only forty-four Mexicans and nine Biloxi Indians were in the group. It is very likely that this report was based on the information obtained from a deserter from Cordova's group. *Telegraph and Texas Register* (Houston), April 10, 1839.

19. Wilbarger, *Indian Depredations,* 153.

20. Col. Edward Burleson to A. Sidney Johnston, Secretary of War, April 3, 1839, *The Morning Star* (Houston), April 11, 1839.

21. Wilbarger, *Indian Depredations,* 153–154. Burleson does not mention this incident in his official report to the secretary of war.

22. *Ibid.,* 154; *The Morning Star,* April 11, 1839.

23. Nance, *After San Jacinto,* 125.

24. Wilbarger, *Indian Depredations,* 155–156.

25. Edward Burleson to M. B. Lamar, April 4, 1838 [1839], Lamar Papers, Doc. 701, TSL-A.

26. A. J. Sowell, *Early Settlers and Indian Fighters of Southwest Texas* (Austin: Ben C. Jones and Company, Printers, 1900), 417.

27. *Ibid.,* 15.

28. On March 9, 1839, General Canalizo, in Matamoros, issued passports to Manuel Flores and Juan Bautista Soto for their trip into Texas. Andrew Jackson Houston Papers, Doc. 4602.19g, TSL-A.

29. A. J. Houston Papers, Doc. 4602.19a, TSL-A.

30. Edward Burleson to A. Sidney Johnston, Secretary of War, May 22, 1839. A. J. Houston Papers, Doc. 4602.19, TSL-A.

31. Nance, *After San Jacinto,* 132–136; Edward Burleson to A. Sidney Johnston, May 22, 1839, *Senate Executive Documents,* 32d [United States] Congress, 2d Session, III, Doc. 14: 29–30.

32. Valentin Canalizo to the chiefs of the Caddoes, Seminoles, Cherokees, and others, February 27, 1839, *Senate Executive Documents,* 32d [United States] Congress, 2d Session, III, Doc. 14: 35; A. J. Houston Papers, Docs. 4602.20-4602.27, TSL-A.

33. Burleson to Johnston, May 22, 1839, *Senate Executive Documents,* 32d [United States] Congress, 2d Session, III, Doc. 14: 29–30.

34. *Laws of the Republic of Texas* (Houston: The Office of the Telegraph, 1838) 2:62-76.

Chapter 2:   EXPULSION OF THE CHEROKEES

1. *Messages of the President, Submitted to Both Houses,* December 21, 1838, Lamar Papers, Doc. 948: 10, TSL-A.

2. *Ibid.,* 11.

3. H. P. N. Gammel, ed., *The Laws of Texas, 1822–1897* (Austin: The Gammel Book Company, 1898) 2:15–20.

4. *Ibid.,* 29–30.

5. Mirabeau B. Lamar to Col. Bowl, and other head men, May 26, 1839, Lamar Papers, Doc. 1297: 125–126, TSL-A.

6. *Ibid.,* 125–127.

7. *Ibid.,* 128.

8. *Richmond Telescope and Register,* July 31, 1839.

9. *Ibid.,* September 4, 1839.

10. John Henry Brown, *Indian Wars and Pioneers of Texas* (Austin: L. E. Daniell, n.d.), 66–69.

11. William Preston Johnston, *The Life of Albert Sidney Johnston* (New York: D. Appleton and Company, Inc., 1879), 108–110.

12. Kelsey H. Douglass to A. Sidney Johnston, July 16, 1839, Lamar Papers, Doc. 1372, TSL-A.

13. K. H. Douglass to A. Sidney Johnston, July 17, 1839, Lamar Papers, Doc. 1373, TSL-A.

14. *Ibid.*; "Extracts From the Report of Genl. K. H. Douglass to the Secy. of War Relative to the Late Cherokee Campaign," Army Papers, correspondence, 1839, Adjutant General Records (RG 401), TSL-A.

15. Wilbarger, *Indian Depredations*, 172.

16. *Richmond Telescope and Register*, September 4, 1839.

17. Webb, *The Texas Rangers*, 54–55; Wilbarger, *Indian Depredations*, 172–173.

Chapter 3: THE COUNCIL HOUSE FIGHT

1. Johnston, *Life of A. S. Johnston*, 115.

2. H. W. Karnes to Albert S. Johnston, January 10, 1840, Records Relating to Indian Affairs (RG 005), Doc. 74, TSL-A.

3. *Ibid.*

4. A. S. Johnston to Lieut. Col. Wm. S. Fisher, January 30, 1840, Records Relating to Indian Affairs (RG 005), Doc. 77, TSL-A.

5. Mildred P. Mayhall, *Indian Wars of Texas* (Waco: The Texian Press, 1965), 21.

6. Frederick C. Chabot, *San Antonio and Its Beginnings* (San Antonio: Artes Graficas Printing Company, 1936), 11, 24, 26, 77–78; Walter P. Webb et al., eds., *Handbook of Texas*, 2:478.

7. Rena Maverick Green, ed., *Memoirs of Mary A. Maverick* (San Antonio: Alamo Printing Company, 1921), 31.

8. Brown, *Indian Wars and Pioneers*, 76–77.

9. Johnston, *Life of A. S. Johnston*, 117.

10. Brown, *Indian Wars and Pioneers*, 77; Report from Colonel Hugh McLeod to M. B. Lamar, March 20, 1840, *Journal of the House*, 5th [Texas] Congress, 1st Session, Appendix, 136–139.

11. Brown, *Indian Wars and Pioneers*, 77.

12. Green, ed., *Memoirs of Mary Maverick*, 33.

13. *Ibid.*, 35.

14. Report from Col. Hugh McLeod to M. B. Lamar, March 20, 1840, *Journals of the House*, 5th [Texas] Congress, 1st Session, Appendix, 138.

15. *Ibid.*

16. Mayhall, *Indian Wars of Texas*, 25–29; Letter from Capt. George T. Howard to Lieut. Col. Wm. S. Fisher, April 6, 1840, "Memoirs of John Salmon Ford," ms, 2:227–228b.

17. Green, ed., *Memoirs of Mary A. Maverick*, 36–37.

18. *Ibid.*, 44.

19. Mayhall, *Indian Wars of Texas*, 25.

Chapter 4: COMANCHE RAIDS ON VICTORIA AND LINNVILLE

1. Sam Houston Dixon, *Romance and Tragedy of Texas History* (Houston: Texas Historical Publishing Company, 1924) 1:266.

2. L. E. Daniell, *Texas: The Country and Its Men* (Austin: L. E. Daniell, n.d.), 49.

3. The number of Indians participating in the Great Comanche Raid seems to vary according to different reports. According to the *Austin City Gazette* of August 12, 1840, the Comanche raiding party consisted of approximately 500 Indians; a later *City Gazette* on August 19 stated that the party consisted of only 200 Indians; John Linn, a citizen of Victoria, reported that there were 600 Indians involved in the raid on Victoria [John J. Linn, *Reminiscences of Fifty Years in Texas* (New York: Sadler and Company, 1883), 338]; Ben McCulloch, who was a major participant in the defeat of the Comanches at Plum Creek, stated that there were close to 1,000 Indians. This estimate is probably too high since it varies quite drastically with the other reports. Victor M. Rose, *The Life and Services of General Ben McCulloch* (Philadelphia: Pictorial Bureau of the Press, 1888), 55.

4. Most accounts of the Comanche raid agree that the first encounter made with the Indians occurred on August 5, although John Holland Jenkins states in his memoirs, printed many years later, that the date was August 6.

5. John Holmes Jenkins, ed., *Recollections of Early Texas: The Memoirs of John Holland Jenkins* (Austin: University of Texas Press, 1958), 60–62.

6. Brown, *Indian Wars and Pioneers*, 79.

7. The Big Hill, located approximately sixteen miles east of Gonzales, is a high elevation on an extended ridge running from the northeast to the southwest. Most Indian parties which penetrated into the lower settlements would usually cross the Gonzales-Columbus road in this area because of the advantage of a high elevation. Brown, *Indian Wars and Pioneers*, 79.

8. *Austin City Gazette*, September 2, 1840.

9. *Ibid.*

10. *Texas Sentinel* (Austin), September 19, 1840; John J. Linn, who was in Victoria at the time of the raid, stated that the attack was made on August 4. Most other accounts disagree with Linn. Since Linn wrote his memoirs forty-three years after the raid, it is understandable that he was mistaken about the date. Linn, *Reminiscences*, 338; *Elizabeth McAnulty Owens: The Story of Her Life* (San Antonio: The Naylor Company, 1936), 19.

11. Linn, *Reminiscences*, 338.

12. *Texas Sentinel* (Austin), September 19, 1840.

13. Linn, *Reminiscences*, 338–339.

14. Brown, *Indian Wars and Pioneers*, 79–80.

15. Linn, *Reminiscences*, 339.

16. *Ibid.*

17. Brown, *Indian Wars and Pioneers*, 80; Mrs. Cyrus Crosby, nee Nancy Darst, was born April 1, 1816, in Missouri. She was the daughter of Jacob C. and Elizabeth Bryan Darst. In January 1831 she arrived in the Green

DeWitt Colony along with her father, her stepmother Margaret Hughes Darst, and her half-brother David S. H. Darst. Jacob C. Darst was one of the "Immortal Thirty-Two" from Gonzales who went to the aid of the Alamo and fell with its defenders on March 6, 1836. *J. W. Franks vs R. D. Hancock*, Texas Supreme Court Records (RG 201), Case File M7406, TSL-A; "Darst" family file, Gonzales County Archives, Gonzales County Courthouse, Gonzales, Texas; *Memorial and Genealogical Record of Southwest Texas* (Chicago: Goodspeed Bros., Publishers, 1894), 82. Nancy Darst was married to Cyrus Crosby in Matagorda County on November 11, 1838. Matagorda County Marriage Records, Book A, 8, County Clerk's Office, Matagorda County Courthouse, Bay City, Texas.

    18. John S. Ford, "Memoirs," ms, 2:233.

    19. Brown, *Indian Wars and Pioneers*, 80.

    20. Linn, *Reminiscences*, 340–341.

    21. *Franks vs Hancock*, Texas Supreme Court Records (RG 201), File M7406, TSL-A.

    22. Linnville was located three and one-half miles northeast of Port Lavaca on Lavaca Bay. The town had been established in 1831 by John J. Linn. The site of the town was in Victoria County, but in 1846 the area became a part of Calhoun County. Webb et al., eds., *Handbook of Texas*, 2:60; Calhoun County Deed Records, Vol. C, 577, County Clerk's Office, Calhoun County Courthouse, Port Lavaca, Texas. After its destruction by the Comanches in 1840, the town was rebuilt and flourished for a few years until its importance as a seaport gave way to a deeper and more favorable harbor at Port Lavaca. Having lost its significance as a seaport the town eventually died out, never to be rebuilt.

    23. *Austin City Gazette*, August 26, 1840.

    24. Ford, "Memoirs," ms. 2:233; "David Brown Moves to Texas," Recollections of Cordelia Brown Harwood as told by Della Paxton Jones, *Gonzales Inquirer*, June 4, 1953; Gilbert Onderdonk, *Stories of Early Texas Life*, ms, 2–5, Gilbert Onderdonk Papers, Barker Texas History Center, University of Texas, Austin.

    25. Linn, *Reminiscences*, 341.

    26. *Austin City Gazette*, August 26, 1840.

    27. Linn, *Reminiscences*, 341–342.

    28. Webb, *The Texas Rangers*, 59.

    29. *Austin City Gazette*, September 2, 1840.

    30. *Ibid.*

    31. Brown, *Indian Wars and Pioneers*, 80.

    32. Mathew Caldwell received his nickname "Old Paint" because of his dark beard which was splotched with white patches. This coloration was reminiscent of a pinto or paint horse. Caldwell was also reported to have had a "tanned complexion" which "was 'interspersed with patches of deathly white.'" George R. Nielson, "Mathew Caldwell," *Southwestern Historical Quarterly* 64, no. 4 (April 1961), 478.

    33. The land owned by Isham Good had initially been a part of the

original William H. Killen grant. On February 28, 1840, Ben McCulloch
purchased from Killen 492 acres for the amount of $3,000. McCulloch im-
mediately sold the land to Isham Good for the same amount. Good was one
of the first pioneers to settle the area. He built a cabin on the old Gonzales-
Austin road. Also known as the "Half-way House," Good's cabin became a
stopping-off place for people traveling between Austin and Gonzales.
Good's house was located three miles east of Plum Creek and approximately
six miles east of Lockhart. *Titles From Gonzales County,* 28–29, County
Clerk's Office, Caldwell County Courthouse, Lockhart, Texas; *Austin City
Gazette,* August 12, 1840; "Life of Isham J. Good," ms, in possession of the
author.

 34. Brown, *Indian Wars and Pioneers,* 80–81.
 35. Rose, *Life of Ben McCulloch,* 56.
 36. Z. N. Morrell, *Flowers and Fruits in the Wilderness: or Forty-six Years
in Texas and Two Winters in Honduras* (Boston: Gould and Lincoln, 1872), 128.
 37. Brown, *Indian Wars and Pioneers,* 81.

Chapter 5: THE BATTLE OF PLUM CREEK

 1. Rose, *Life of Ben McCulloch,* 62–63.
 2. *Journal of the House,* 5th [Texas] Congress, 1st Session, Appendix,
141; Brown, *Indian Wars and Pioneers,* 81.
 3. Rose, *Life of Ben McCulloch,* 63.
 4. Jenkins, *Recollections of Early Texas,* 64–65.
 5. Morrell, *Flowers and Fruits,* 129. This chief is mentioned in most reports and accounts of the Battle of Plum Creek. One account states that the
Indian was in full dress except for his pants. He wore his "fine calf boots on
over his naked legs, and wore his coat on backwards, buttoned up to the
back of his neck." Sowell, *Early Settlers and Indian Fighters,* 19.
 6. Rose, *Life of Ben McCulloch,* 63.
 7. This initial contact between the Texans and the Indians occurred
on a large open prairie known today as Comanche Flats. The area is located
five miles southeast of Lockhart. A. A. Ross, M.D. to R. M. Farrar, May
28, 1932, letter in possession of author; United States Department of the Interior, Geological Survey Map, McMahan Quadrangle, 1963.
 8. Jenkins, *Recollections of Early Texas,* 63–64.
 9. *Ibid.,* 68. The man killed in this unfortunate incident was Mr.
DeWolf, a member of the Border Guards. Ford, "Memoirs," ms, 2:230. The
Border Guards was an organization which was created for the defense of the
frontier area. It was stationed in San Antonio as a part of Henry W.
Karnes's unit. The group was disbanded at the request of Hugh McLeod,
who felt that the guard was "worthless." The frontier defense force was re-
organized in 1840 and was commanded by James D. Cocke. Nance, *After San
Jacinto,* 329, 532.
 10. A. A. Ross to R. M. Farrar, May 28, 1932.
 11. Brown, *Indian Wars and Pioneers,* 81.
 12. There was a superstition among the Comanches that if they were

able to encircle and run around a force, "they could certainly vanquish it."
Jenkins, *Recollections of Early Texas*, 64.

    13. Morrell, *Flowers and Fruits*, 129–130.

    14. Brown, *Indian Wars and Pioneers*, 82.

    15. Rose, *Life of Ben McCulloch*, 64.

    16. *Journal of the House*, 5th [Texas] Congress, 1st Session, Appendix, 142.

    17. Jenkins, *Recollections of Early Texas*, 65; Brown, *Indian Wars and Pioneers*, 82.

    18. Catherine W. McDowell, ed., *Now You Hear My Horn: The Journal of James Wilson Nichols, 1820–1887* (Austin and London: University of Texas Press, 1967), 64–65.

    19. Andrew Jackson Sowell, *Rangers and Pioneers of Texas* (San Antonio: Shepard Brothers and Company, 1884), 207. In 1838 Alonzo B. Sweitzer was elected to the Texas Congress to represent the citizens of the Gonzales area "but failed to give general satisfaction." When the elections of 1839 were held, many of the dissatisfied people of Gonzales persuaded Ben McCulloch to run for the office held by Sweitzer. The ensuing campaign became heated, and bitter feelings arose between the two candidates. These feelings were carried over after McCulloch won a narrow margin victory and finally came to a head when Sweitzer sent a challenge to McCulloch by Reuben Ross. McCulloch refused to accept Sweitzer's challenge "on the ground that he was not a gentleman." Considering this a personal insult, Ross offered to stand in Sweitzer's stead. McCulloch agreed to this arrangement and in the duel was seriously wounded in the arm by Ross. Thus matters stood until Christmas of 1839. At a Christmas Eve dance being attended by a number of young couples in Gonzales, Ross and Sweitzer entered, although uninvited and "both somewhat intoxicated." The party continued "until the conduct of Colonel Ross became so gross" that some of the young men ushered the ladies into a separate room to spare them further insult. Henry McCulloch physically prevented Ross from entering the other room, and Ross drew his pistols. At the same moment Henry McCulloch also drew a pistol and fired one shot into Ross's breast, killing him instantly. Bitter personal feelings remained between Sweitzer and the McCullochs long after this incident, and these feelings were carried into battle on August 12, 1840. Secretary of State Election Returns for Gonzales County, 1839, (RG 307), TSL-A; *Weekly Dallas Herald*, August 22, 1874.

    20. Sowell, *Rangers and Pioneers of Texas*, 209.

    21. *Ibid.*; Sowell, *Early Settlers and Indian Fighters*, 19.

    22. Brazos [pseud.], *The Life of Robert Hall* (Austin: Ben C. Jones and Company, Printers, 1898), 52.

    23. Brown, *Indian Wars and Pioneers*, 82; Jenkins, *Recollections of Early Texas*, 67–68.

    24. Sowell, *Rangers and Pioneers*, 210; McDowell, ed., *Now You Hear My Horn*, 62, 74–75; Jenkins, *Recollections of Early Texas*, 65–66; Samuel H. Reid, his heirs E. Reid and children, December 12, 1855, Memorials and Petitions, (RG 100), TSL-A; Brazos, *Life of Robert Hall*, 50.

25. Brown, *Indian Wars and Pioneers*, 82; Brazos, *Life of Robert Hall*, 50–51. Some accounts of the Battle of Plum Creek state that Mrs. Watts was the only captive recovered, but the *Austin City Gazette* of August 19, 1840, reported that Mrs. Watts, the Negro woman, and the Negro child were rescued.

26. Juliet Constance Watts, nee Ewing, was born in Ireland and emigrated to Texas with her brother, William G. Ewing, on September 17, 1839. She was married to Hugh O. Watts on July 18, 1840. They had been married for only twenty-one days when Major Watts was killed by the Indians in the raid on Linnville. Juliet Watts later married James M. Stanton on November 14, 1842. This marriage ended in a divorce on September 22, 1847. Mrs. Stanton was the proprietress of the Stanton Hotel in Port Lavaca when she married Dr. J. R. Fretwell on May 23, 1852. They continued to operate the hotel until her death on August 3, 1878. *Seventh Census of the United States, 1850*, Calhoun County, Texas, household #145, p. 498; Republic of Texas Payments for Service, Unpaid Claims, "Juliet C. Stanton," (RG 304), TSL-A; Victoria County Marriage Records, 1:2,4, County Clerk's Office, Victoria County Courthouse, Victoria, Texas; District Court Minutes, Vol. A, p. 10, District Clerk's Office, Calhoun County Courthouse, Port Lavaca, Texas; *The Wave* (Port Lavaca), December 11, 1975; *Indianola Bulletin*, May 27, 1852; Wilbarger, *Indian Depredations*, 33; *Victoria Advocate*, August 17, 1878.

27. Sowell, *Early Settlers and Indian Fighters*, 418–419; Recollections of Cordelia Brown Harwood, *Gonzales Inquirer*, June 4, 1953; Morrell, *Flowers and Fruits*, 130–131; Mayhall, *Indian Wars of Texas*, 39.

28. E. W. Winkler, ed., *Manuscript Letters and Documents of Early Texians, 1821–1845* (Austin: The Steck Company, 1937), 237; Mayhall, *Indian Wars of Texas*, 29.

29. Sowell, *Rangers and Pioneers*, 207–208.

30. *Austin City Gazette*, August 19, 1840; Jenkins, *Recollections of Early Texas*, 67–68; Brazos, *Life of Robert Hall*, 53.

31. Interview with William Fulps, August 10, 1966, Lockhart, Texas.

32. The approximate location of Nancy Crosby's burial is one and a half miles west of Lockhart. *Lockhart Morning Courier* (Special Edition), October 5, 1908.

33. A. S. Ruthven, ed., *Proceedings of the Grand Lodge of Texas, 1837–1857* (Galveston: Richardson and Company, News Office, 1857), 1:392.

34. Brown, *Indian Wars and Pioneers*, 82.

35. Brazos, *Life of Robert Hall*, 52–53; A. J. Sowell states that the Tonkawas cut off only the hands and feet of the Comanches. They also cut one large Indian "into strips and hung the pieces on a rope." Sowell, *Early Settlers and Indian Fighters*, 314. The Comanches were the mortal enemies of the Tonkawas. "Eating portions of the enemy 'killed' the spirit of the enemy and by a belief in associative magic strengthened the power of the consumer." Mayhall, *Indian Wars of Texas*, 201.

36. *Journal of the House*, 5th [Texas] Congress, 1st Session, Appendix, 142–144; *Austin City Gazette*, August 19, 1840; Brazos, *Life of Robert Hall*, 52.

37. Sowell, *Rangers and Pioneers of Texas,* 210; Jenkins, *Recollections of Early Texas,* 65. Another man who claimed to have been wounded in the Battle of Plum Creek was Nelson Lee. Nelson Lee, *Three Years Among the Comanches* (Albany, NY: B. Taylor, 1859), 26. Nichols states that among the wounded were Henry C. Winchel and James Gipson. McDowell, ed., *Now You Hear My Horn,* 70.

38. Although it was reported that one of the seven wounded men at the Battle of Plum Creek was mortally wounded, this was an error. Late in the day of the battle when General Huston made his official report of the action to the secretary of war, it was believed that Samuel Hutchinson Reed had been mortally wounded. Reed's wound was caused by an arrow which entered "under the point of the left shoulder blade" and "passed through his lungs and lodged against his right breastbone to the depth of about nine inches from which wound it was thought by all present that he must immediately die but it was not the case." Maj. Gen. Felix Huston's Report of Plum Creek Battle, August 12, 1840, Doc. 1966, A. J. Houston Papers, TSL-A; Samuel H. Reid, his heirs E. Reid and children, December 12, 1855, Memorials and Petitions, (RG 100), TSL-A.

39. Brazos, *Life of Robert Hall,* 53.

Chapter 6:   MOORE'S VICTORY ON THE UPPER COLORADO

1. Wilbarger, *Indian Depredations,* 184.

2. *Austin City Gazette,* September 2, 1840.

3. Col. John H. Moore's official report to the secretary of war, *Telegraph and Texas Register,* November 18, 1840. Harrell, who had died on October 16, had developed a sore throat from the inclement weather conditions. The sore throat then developed into quinsy, an illness similar to diphtheria. Jenkins, *Recollections of Early Texas,* 174.

4. Moore's official report, *Telegraph and Texas Register,* November 18, 1840. John Jenkins states that the Texans discovered, along the Red Fork of the Colorado, many rocks "with curious pictures and hieroglyphics" painted on them. Further on, the men discovered pecan hulls which had recently been scattered on the ground. Jenkins, *Recollections of Early Texas,* 171.

5. Moore's official report, *Telegraph and Texas Register,* November 18, 1840; Jenkins, *Recollections of Early Texas,* 171–172.

6. Moore's official report, *Telegraph and Texas Register,* November 18, 1840. Clarke L. Owen was later killed in the Battle of Shiloh in 1862. Capt. Nicholas Dawson "commanded and fell at the Dawson Massacre in 1842." Brown, *Indian Wars and Pioneers,* 83.

7. Moore's official report, *Telegraph and Texas Register,* November 18, 1840; Wilbarger, *Indian Depredations,* 184–185.

8. Moore's official report, *Telegraph and Texas Register,* November 18, 1840.

9. Brown, *Indian Wars and Pioneers,* 84; Mayhall, *Indian Wars of Texas,* 41.

10. Jenkins, *Recollections of Early Texas,* 172–173.

11. Moore's official report, *Telegraph and Texas Register,* November 18, 1840. In this fight the Comanche chief Machochochomochouch was killed. Jenkins, *Recollections of Early Texas,* 173. Brown states that only two warriors escaped during the fight. He also says that "every warrior was killed, excepting a few old men and one or two young men, who surrendered and were spared." Brown, *Indian Wars and Pioneers,* 83.

12. Moore's official report, *Telegraph and Texas Register,* November 18, 1840.

13. *Ibid.*

14. Brown, *Indian Wars and Pioneers,* 84.

15. Moore's official report, *Telegraph and Texas Register,* November 18, 1840; Jenkins, *Recollections of Early Texas,* 173.

16. Moore's official report, *Telegraph and Texas Register,* November 18, 1840.

17. Jenkins, *Recollections of Early Texas,* 173–174.

18. *Ibid.,* 174.

19. *Ibid.,* 174–175.

20. *Ibid.,* 175–176.

Chapter 7: RESULTS OF THE COMANCHE DEFEAT

1. Georgia J. Burleson, ed., *The Life and Writings of Rufus C. Burleson* (n.p., 1901), 839–840.

2. Webb, *The Texas Rangers,* 58. Jenkins states that the Indians "were supposed to have been guided by Mexicans." Jenkins, *Recollections of Early Texas,* 61.

3. Linn, *Reminiscences,* 339; Brown, *Indian Wars and Pioneers,* 79–80.

4. Mayhall, *Indian Wars of Texas,* 33.

5. Rose, *Life of Ben McCulloch,* 61.

6. Walter Webb et al., eds., *Handbook of Texas,* 2:460.

7. Nance, *After San Jacinto,* 252.

8. *Ibid.,* 260–267; *Telegraph and Texas Register,* April 29, 1840.

9. William S. Fisher to Hugh McLeod, April 8, 1840, *Austin City Gazette,* April 15, 1840.

10. *Telegraph and Texas Register,* April 29, 1840; Jesús Cárdenas to M. B. Lamar, April 8, 1840, Lamar Papers, Doc. 1765, TSL-A.

11. Samuel A. Plummer to M. B. Lamar, April 25, 1840, Lamar Papers, Doc. 1789, TSL-A; *Telegraph and Texas Register,* April 29, 1840.

12. Samuel A. Plummer to M. B. Lamar, April 25, 1840, Lamar Papers, Doc. 1789, TSL-A.

13. *Telegraph and Texas Register,* April 29, 1840.

14. James N. Smith, "Autobiography," 3:218, ms, Barker Texas History Center, University of Texas, Austin.

15. Linn, *Reminiscences,* 339, 341–342.

16. Brown, *Indian Wars and Pioneers,* 80; Rose, *Life of Ben McCulloch,* 55-56.

17. Jenkins, *Recollections of Early Texas,* 64.

18. Brazos, *Life of Robert Hall*, 51.

19. *Journal of the House,* 5th [Texas] Congress, 1st Session, Appendix, 144.

20. Dixon, *Romance and Tragedy*, 268–269.

21. Captain Flack, *The Texan Rifle Hunter* (London: John Maxwell and Company, 1866), 133.

22. *Ibid.*

23. Dixon, *Romance and Tragedy*, 269.

24. *Austin City Gazette,* September 2, 1840; Brown, *Indian Wars and Pioneers,* 80.

25. *Journal of the House,* 5th [Texas] Congress, 1st Session, Appendix, 141–142.

26. Moore's official report, *Telegraph and Texas Register,* November 18, 1840.

27. *San Antonio Light,* January 15, 1966.

28. *Journal of the House,* 5th [Texas] Congress, 1st Session, Appendix, 142.

29. Moore's official report, *Telegraph and Texas Register,* November 18, 1840.

30. John C. Hays exhibited his leadership both in the Texas Rangers and in the Mexican War. Webb, *The Texas Rangers,* 69, 94; Ben McCulloch commanded a company of Texans in the Mexican War. He later attained the rank of brigadier general and died in the Battle of Elk Horn Tavern, Arkansas. Webb, *The Texas Rangers,* 94; Wilbarger, *Indian Depredations,* 290; Henry McCulloch also participated in the Mexican War and the Civil War. Wilbarger, *Indian Depredations,* 612–613; Lt. Clarke L. Owen was killed in the Battle of Shiloh, 1862. He had attained the rank of captain. Brown, *Indian Wars and Pioneers,* 83.

31. James T. DeShields, *Border Wars of Texas* (Tioga, Texas: Herald Company, 1912), 320.

Bibliography

A. Primary Sources

1. Public Documents
   a. Manuscripts

Adjutant General Records (RG 401). Army Papers (Texas). Texas State Library, Archives Division, Austin, Texas.

————. Military Rolls (Republic). Texas State Library, Archives Division, Austin, Texas.

Comptroller's Audited Claims (RG 304). Texas State Library, Archives Division, Austin, Texas.

Consular Dispatches (Texas), 1837–1839 (Matamoros). Barker Texas History Center, University of Texas, Austin.

County Records. Calhoun County Deed Records. County Clerk's Office, Calhoun County Courthouse, Port Lavaca, Texas.

————. Matagorda County Marriage Records. County Clerk's Office, Matagorda County Courthouse, Bay City, Texas.

————. *Titles From Gonzales County.* Caldwell County Deed Records, County Clerk's Office, Caldwell County Courthouse, Lockhart, Texas.

————. Victoria County Marriage Records. County Clerk's Office, Victoria County Courthouse, Victoria, Texas.

————. Victoria County Probate Records. County Clerk's Office, Victoria County Courthouse, Victoria, Texas.

District Records. District Court Minutes. District Clerk's Office, Calhoun County Courthouse, Port Lavaca, Texas.

Memorials and Petitions (RG 100). Texas State Library, Archives Division, Austin, Texas.

Records Relating to Indian Affairs (RG 005). Series I. Texas State Library, Archives Division, Austin, Texas.

Secretary of State (RG 307). Department of State Letter Book, No. 1 (November 1836–January 1842). Texas State Library, Archives Division, Austin, Texas.

————. Election Returns. Gonzales County (1839). Texas State Library, Archives Division, Austin, Texas.

————. Executive Record Book. Sam Houston and M. B. Lamar, 1836–1841. Texas State Library, Archives Division, Austin, Texas.

————. Executive Record Book. M. B. Lamar, 1838–1841. Texas State Library, Archives Division, Austin, Texas.

Texas Supreme Court Records (RG 201). *J. W. Franks vs R. D. Hancock* (M7406). Texas State Library, Archives Division, Austin, Texas.

Treasurer's Records (RG 310). Customs House Records. Texas State Library, Archives Division, Austin, Texas.

b. Printed

Day, James, and Dorman Winfrey, eds. *The Indian Papers of Texas and the Southwest.* 5 vols. Austin: Texas State Library, 1959–66.

Gammel, H. P. N., ed. *The Laws of Texas, 1822–1897.* 10 vols. Austin: The Gammel Book Company, 1898.

Laws of the Republic of Texas. 2 vols. Houston: Office of the Telegraph, 1838.

Miracle, Pedro Julian. "Memorandum Book [of Pedro Julian Miracle]," in "Report of the Secretary of State . . . Relative to the Encroachments of the Indians of the United States upon the Territories of Mexico, Washington, January 11, 1853," *Senate Executive Documents*, 32d Congress, 2d Session, No. 14.

Ruthven, A. S., ed. *Proceedings of the Grand Lodge of Texas, 1837–1857.* Galveston: Richardson and Company, News Office, 1857.

Texas Congress. *Journal of the House of Representatives of the Republic of Texas: First Congress, Second Session.* Houston: Telegraph Office, 1838.

————. *Journals of the House of Representatives of the Republic of Texas: Fifth Congress, First Session, Appendix.* [Austin]: Gazette Office, 1841.

Texas War Department. *Annual Report of the Secretary of War, November 1839. Printed by order of Congress.* Austin: Whiting's Press 1839.

United States Census. *Seventh Census of the United States, 1850.* Calhoun County, Texas.

United States Congress. *Senate Executive Documents*, 25th Congress, 2d Session, vol. XII, no. 351.

————. *Senate Executive Documents*, 32d Congress, 2d Session, vol. III, no. 14.

2. Private Papers, Letters, and Memoirs

a. Manuscripts and Typescripts

Bell, Thomas W. Papers. Barker Texas History Center, University of Texas, Austin.

Billingsley, Jesse. Papers. Barker Texas History Center, University of Texas, Austin.

Brown, John Henry. Papers. Barker Texas History Center, University of Texas, Austin.

Ford, John S. "Memoirs." 7 vols. MS. Texas State Library, Archives Division, Austin, Texas.

Houston, Andrew Jackson. Papers. Texas State Library, Archives Division, Austin, Texas.

James, Vinton L. "Old Times in San Antonio." MS. Barker Texas History Center, University of Texas, Austin.

Jenkins, John Holland, Sr. "Personal Reminiscences of Texas History Relating to Bastrop County, 1828–1847." TS. Barker Texas History Center, University of Texas, Austin.

Johnston, Albert Sidney. Letters. MS. Texas State Library, Archives Division, Austin, Texas.

Lamar, Mirabeau Buonaparte. Papers. Texas State Library, Archives Division, Austin, Texas.

Menefee, John S. Papers. Barker Texas History Center, University of Texas, Austin.

Onderdonk, Gilbert. Papers. Barker Texas History Center, University of Texas, Austin.

Rogers, Samuel C. A. "Reminiscences of Samuel C. A. Rogers." TS. Barker Texas History Center, University of Texas, Austin.

Ross, Dr. A. A. Letter to R. M. Farrar, May 28, 1932. In possession of Donaly E. Brice, Lockhart, Texas.

Ross, Reuben. Papers. Barker Texas History Center. University of Texas, Austin.

Smith, James N. "Autobiography." MS. Barker Texas History Center, University of Texas, Austin.

Vandale, Earl. Collection. Barker Texas History Center, University of Texas, Austin.

b. Printed

Brazos [pseud.]. *The Life of Robert Hall.* Austin: Ben C. Jones and Company, Printers, 1898.

Brown, John Henry. *Indian Wars and Pioneers of Texas.* Austin: L. E. Daniell, [n.d.].

Burleson, Georgia J., ed. *The Life and Writings of Rufus C. Burleson.* [n.p.]: 1901.

Elizabeth McAnulty Owens: The Story of Her Life. San Antonio: The Naylor Company, 1936.

Flack, Captain. *The Texan Rifle Hunter: or Field Sports on the Prairie.* London: John Maxwell and Company, 1866.

Green, Rena Maverick, ed. *Memoirs of Mary A. Maverick: Arranged by Mary A. Maverick and Her Son George Madison Maverick.* San Antonio: Alamo Printing Company, 1921.

Gulick, Jr., Charles Adams, ed. *The Papers of Mirabeau Buonaparte Lamar.* 6 vols. Austin: A. C. Baldwin and Sons, Printers, 1922.

Jenkins, John Holmes, ed. *Recollections of Early Texas: The Memoirs of John Holland Jenkins.* Austin: University of Texas Press, 1958.

Kennedy, William. *Texas: The Rise, Progress, and Prospects of the Republic of Texas.* 2d ed. 2 vols. London: R. Hastings, 1841.

Lee, Nelson. *Three Years Among the Comanches.* Albany, NY: B. Taylor, 1859.

Linn, John J. *Reminiscences of Fifty Years in Texas.* New York: Sadler and Company, 1883.

McDowell, Catherine W., ed. *Now You Hear My Horn: The Journal of James Wilson Nichols, 1820–1887.* Austin and London: University of Texas Press, 1967.

Morrell Z. N. *Flowers and Fruits in the Wilderness: or Forty-six Years in Texas and Two Winters in Honduras.* Boston: Gould and Lincoln, 1872.

Smith, Cornelius C. *William Sanders Oury: History-maker of the Southwest.* Tucson: Arizona University Press, 1967.

Winkler, E. W., ed. *Manuscript Letters and Documents of Early Texians, 1821–1845.* Austin: The Steck Company, 1937.

3. Maps

Caldwell County. Austin: General Land Office, 1896.

Cherokee Land Grant in East Texas. Texas State Library, Archives Division, Austin, Texas.

Comanche Country and Adjacent Territory, 1840. Printed in *The Comanche Barrier to South Plains Settlement* by Rupert N. Richardson.

Connected Map of the County of Victoria. Made from the surveys of Jas. Kerr, J. M. J. Carbajal and B. Lockhart, Esqr's., by Edward Lynn, surveyor of Victoria County. Date prior to Nov. 7, 1838. Austin: General Land Office.

McMahan Quadrangle, Texas, Caldwell County. Denver: United States Geological Survey, U.S. Department of Interior, 1963.

4. Newspapers

Austin City Gazette, August–November, 1840.

Colorado Gazette and Advertiser (Matagorda), August–November, 1840.

Gonzales Inquirer, June 4, 1953.

Indianola Bulletin, May 27, 1852.

Morning Courier (Lockhart), October 5, 1908.

Lockhart Post-Register, August 1964–August 1966.

Morning Star, The (Houston), 1839.

Richmond Telescope and Register, July–September, 1839.

San Antonio Light, January 15, 1966.

Telegraph and Texas Register (Houston), 1839–1841.

Texas Sentinel (Austin), August 1840–March 1841.

Victoria Advocate, August 17, 1878.

Wave, The (Port Lavaca), December 11, 1975.

Weekly Dallas Herald, August 22, 1874.

B. Secondary Sources

1. Manuscripts and Typescripts

Brice, Donaly E. "The Great Comanche Raid of 1840: Its Causes and Results." Master's thesis, Sam Houston State University, 1968.

Brown, Frank. "Annals of Travis County and the City of Austin." TS. Texas State Library, Archives Division, Austin, Texas.

Corkran, Charles Wesley. "John Henry Moore, 1800–1880." Master's thesis, University of Texas, 1964.

"Darst" family file. Gonzales County Archives. Gonzales County Courthouse, Gonzales, Texas.

Huson, Hobart. "Iron Men: A History of the Republic of the Rio

Grande and the Federalist War in Northern Mexico." MS. Texas State Library, Archives Division, Austin, Texas.

Lackman, Howard. "George Thomas Howard, Texas Frontiersman." Ph.D. dissertation, University of Texas, 1954.

"Life of Isham J. Good." TS presenting a brief sketch of the life of Isham J. Good. In possession of Donaly E. Brice, Lockhart, Texas.

O'Banion, Maurine M. "The History of Caldwell County." Master's thesis, University of Texas, 1931.

Urich, Frank E. "Felix Huston the Unknown: A Brief Biography, 1800–1857." TS in Barker Texas History Center, University of Texas, Austin.

Vigness, David Martell. "The Republic of the Rio Grande: An Example of Separatism in Northern Mexico." Ph.D. dissertation, University of Texas, 1951.

2. Printed
   a. Books

Bancroft, Hubert Howe. *A History of the North Mexican States and Texas*. 2 vols. San Francisco: The History Company, Publishers, 1889.

Brown, John Henry. *History of Texas, From 1685 to 1892*. 2 vols. St. Louis: L. E. Daniell, [1892–1893].

Chabot, Frederick C. *San Antonio and Its Beginnings*. San Antonio: Artes Graficas Printing Company, 1936.

Christian, Asa Kyrus. *Mirabeau Buonaparte Lamar*. Austin: Von Boeckmann-Jones Company, Printers, 1922.

Clarke, Mary Whatley. *Chief Bowles and the Texas Cherokees*. Norman: University of Oklahoma Press, 1971.

Connor, Seymour V. *Adventure in Glory*. Vol. III of *The Saga of Texas Series*. Edited by Seymour Connor. 6 vols. Austin: Steck-Vaughn Company, 1965.

———, et. al. *Battles of Texas*. Waco: Texian Press, 1967.

Daniell, L. E. *Texas: The Country and Its Men*. Austin: L. E. Daniell, [n.d.].

DeShields, James T. *Border Wars of Texas: Being an Authentic and Popular Account, in Chronological Order, of the Long and Bitter Conflict Waged Between Savage Indian Tribes and the Pioneer Settlers of Texas*. Tioga, Texas: Herald Company, 1912.

Dixon, Sam Houston. *Romance and Tragedy of Texas History: Being a Record of Many Thrilling Events in Texas History Under Spanish, Mexican and Anglo-Saxon Rule*. Houston: Texas Historical Publishing Company, 1924.

Fehrenbach, T. R. *Comanches: The Destruction of a People*. New York: Alfred A. Knopf, 1974.

———. *Lone Star: A History of Texas and the Texans*. New York: Macmillan Company, 1968.

Hicks, John D. *The Federal Union: A History of the United States to 1865*. Cambridge, MA: Houghton Mifflin Company, Riverside Press, 1952.

Huson, Hobart. *District Judges of Refugio County.* Refugio, Texas: Refugio Timely Remarks, 1941.

Johnston, William Preston. *The Life of General Albert Sidney Johnston: Embracing His Services in the Armies of the United States, the Republic of Texas, and the Confederate States.* New York: D. Appleton and Company, Inc., 1879.

Marshall, Thomas Maitland. *A History of the Western Boundary of the Louisiana Purchase, 1819–1841.* Berkeley: University of California Press, 1914.

Mayhall, Mildred P. *Indian Wars of Texas.* Waco: Texian Press, 1965.

Memorial and Genealogical Record of Southwest Texas. Chicago: Goodspeed Bros., Publishers, 1894.

Nance, Joseph Milton. *After San Jacinto: The Texas-Mexican Frontier, 1836–1841.* Austin: University of Texas Press, 1963.

Oates, Stephen B., ed. *Rip Ford's Texas: By John Salmon Ford.* Austin: University of Texas Press, 1963.

Richardson, Rupert N. *Texas: The Lone Star State.* Englewood Cliffs, NJ: Prentice-Hall, Inc., 1958.

———. *The Comanche Barrier to South Plains Settlement.* Glendale, CA: Arthur H. Clarke Company, 1938.

Rose, Victor M. *The Life and Services of General Ben McCulloch.* Philadelphia: Pictorial Bureau of the Press, 1888.

Sowell, A. J. *Early Settlers and Indian Fighters of Southwest Texas.* Austin: Ben C. Jones and Company, Printers, 1900.

———. *Rangers and Pioneers of Texas.* San Antonio: Shepard Brothers and Company, 1884.

Syers, William Edward. *Off the Beaten Trail.* 3 vols. Fort Worth: F. L. Motheral Company, 1963.

Webb, Walter Prescott. *The Texas Rangers: A Century of Frontier Defense.* Austin: University of Texas Press, 1935.

———, H. Bailey Carroll, and Eldon S. Branda, eds. *The Handbook of Texas.* 3 vols. Austin: Texas State Historical Association, 1952, 1976.

Wilbarger, J. W. *Indian Depredations in Texas.* Austin: Hutchings Printing House, 1889.

Winfrey, Dorman H. *Chief Bowles of the Texas Cherokees.* Oklahoma City: Oklahoma Historical Society, 1953. Reprint from *Chronicles of Oklahoma* 32, no. I.

Wooten, Dudley G. *A Comprehensive History of Texas, 1685–1897.* 2 vols. Dallas: W. G. Scarff, 1898.

Wortham, Louis J. *A History of Texas From Wilderness to Commonwealth.* 5 vols. Fort Worth: Wortham-Molyneaux Company, 1924.

Yoakum, Henderson. *History of Texas From Its First Settlement in 1685 to Its Annexation to the United States in 1846.* 2 vols. New York: J. S. Redfield, 1855.

b. Articles

Gunn, Jack W. "Ben McCulloch: A Big Captain." *Southwestern Historical Quarterly* 58 (July 1954): 3–4.

Muckleroy, Anna. "The Indian Policy of the Republic of Texas." *Southwestern Historical Quarterly* 26 (1922–1923): 26–145.

Nielson, George R. "Mathew Caldwell." *Southwestern Historical Quarterly* 64 (April 1961): 478–489.

Vigness, David M. "Relations of the Republic of Texas and the Republic of the Rio Grande." *Southwestern Historical Quarterly* 57 (July 1953–April 1954): 312–321.

Weaver, Bobby D. "Relations Between the Comanche Indians and the Republic of Texas." *Panhandle-Plains Historical Review* 53 (1980): 17–33.

Woldert, Albert. "The Last of the Cherokees in Texas, and the Life and Death of Chief Bowles." *Chronicles of Oklahoma* 1 (June 1923): 179–226.

3. Interviews

William Fulps, with author, August 10, 1966, Lockhart, Texas.

Index

Jones, W. J., 17–18,
  see also Texas militia
K
Karnes, Henry W., 21–22
Kaufman, David S., 19
Keene, Richard H., 71
Kelley, Springs, 41
Kickapoo Indians, 9
Killen, William H.,
  land grant of, 96–97
Kiowa Indians,
  attacking with Comanches,
    see Comanche Raid of 1840
Kornegay, David S., 71
Kraatz, Lewis, 68
L
Lamar, Mirabeau B.:
  accusing Cherokees of alliance
    with Mexicans, 16–17
  anti-Indian policy, 2–3, 15–16
  appointing commissioners for
    negotiating with Chero-
    kees, 17–18
  bill for formation of mounted
    volunteers, 16
  bill providing for offensive oper-
    ations against, 15–16
  declaring null an 1836 contract
    with Cherokees, 16
  expulsion of Cherokees, 15–20
  inaugural address, 1–2, 15
  involvement in removal of
    Creek Indians from
    Georgia, 2
  letters to Chief Bowles, 16–17
  negotiating for peaceful removal
    of Cherokees, 14
  ordering attack on Cherokees,
    18
  ordering construction of fort in
    vicinity of Cherokee Na-
    tion, 17
land law enacted, 13–14
Landrum, Willis H., command of,
  18,
  see also Texas militia
Lavaca company,
  skirmish at Garcitas Creek, 34
Lavaca volunteers, 35

Lawrence, Joseph, 69, 71
Lee, Nelson, 69
Lester, James, 67
Linn, John J.:
  establishment of Linnville, 96
  estimate of Indians participat-
    ing in Victoria raids, 81
  fixing date of Victoria raid, 81
Linnville:
  as point of entry for goods des-
    tined for Victoria, 60
  Comanche raid at, 4, 31–33,
    58–60
    assistance from Mexicans,
      58–60
    burning of town, 32–33
    casualties, 32
    efforts of Indians to avoid
      fighting, 61
    factors leading to, 60
    plunder taken, 32–33, 58
    reasons for raid, 59
    retreat by citizens, 32
  establishment of, 82
Lipan Indians, 50–51
Litton, Addison, 69
Litton, Frank M., 69
Lloyd, Richard J., 67
Lockhart, Matilda, 22–23, 26
Long, William, 71
Longley, James P., 71
Lubbock, Thomas S., 71
Lynch, Addison, 71
Lynch, John L., 20, 67
Lyons, DeWitt C., 71
M
Mabry, James L., 67
Machochochomochouch, Chief,
  101
Magill, James P., 69
Magill, William Harrison, 69
Matamoros,
  Cherokee delegation at, 6–7
Mayfield, James S., 17–18
McAnnelly, Pleasant, 71
McCoy, John, 69
McCulloch, Benjamin:
  arrival at Gonzales to solicit
    aid, 35–36